Transmodern Cinema and Decolonial Film Theory

Transmodern Cinema and Decolonial Film Theory

A Study of Youssef Chahine's al-Maṣīr

Robert K. Beshara

BLOOMSBURY ACADEMIC

NEW YORK · LONDON · OXFORD · NEW DELHI · SYDNEY

BLOOMSBURY ACADEMIC
Bloomsbury Publishing Inc
1385 Broadway, New York, NY 10018, USA
50 Bedford Square, London, WC1B 3DP, UK
29 Earlsfort Terrace, Dublin 2, Ireland

BLOOMSBURY, BLOOMSBURY ACADEMIC and the Diana logo are trademarks of
Bloomsbury Publishing Plc

First published in the United States of America 2024

Copyright © Robert K. Beshara, 2024

For legal purposes the Acknowledgments on p. viii constitute an extension of this
copyright page.

Cover design: Eleanor Rose
Cover image: Nour El-Sherif in *al-Maṣīr*, 1997, dir.
Youssef Chahine © Misr International Films

All rights reserved. No part of this publication may be reproduced or transmitted
in any form or by any means, electronic or mechanical, including photocopying,
recording, or any information storage or retrieval system, without prior
permission in writing from the publishers.

Bloomsbury Publishing Inc does not have any control over, or responsibility for, any
third-party websites referred to or in this book. All internet addresses given in this
book were correct at the time of going to press. The author and publisher regret any
inconvenience caused if addresses have changed or sites have ceased to exist,
but can accept no responsibility for any such changes.

A catalog record for this book is available from the Library of Congress.

ISBN: HB: 978-1-5013-8511-7
ePDF: 978-1-5013-8509-4
eBook: 978-1-5013-8510-0

Typeset by Newgen KnowledgeWorks Pvt. Ltd., Chennai, India

To find out more about our authors and books visit www.bloomsbury.com
and sign up for our newsletters.

This book is dedicated to my parents—my father Khairy and my mother Monika—because they instilled a passion for cinema in me, which, in the end, is a mimetic passion for life itself. It is also dedicated to my lovely wife, Cony, who enjoys experiencing filmic masterpieces with me! Finally, the book is in memory of Afaf Mardini.

Contents

Acknowledgments	viii
Introduction	1
Part 1 Decolonial Film Theory	25
1 Decolonial Film Theory	27
Part 2 Decoloniality and *al-Maṣīr*	75
2 Ibn Rushd (1126–1198)	77
3 Youssef Chahine (1926–2008)	99
4 The Decoloniality of Poetics: *al-Maṣīr* (1997)	131
Conclusion: The Future of Decolonial Film Theory	153
Further Reading on Youssef Chahine	159
Youssef Chahine's Filmography	161
References	163
Index	175

Acknowledgments

First, I would like to acknowledge Katie Gallof, Film and Media Studies editor at Bloomsbury, for allowing me to introduce a slice of Egyptian cinema to a broad English-speaking audience. Second, I appreciate Marianne Khoury's help, on behalf of Misr International Films, in providing me with the photos used in the book.

Introduction

Before I begin, I wish to express that I conceived of this book as an introduction to both decolonial theory in general and Youssef Chahine's cinema in particular. While there are several books on decolonial aesthetics, there was not a single book on decolonial cinema, which is why I was compelled to invent *decolonial film theory*. Similarly, there are only two books, in the English language, on Chahine: Ibrahim Fawal's (2001) *Youssef Chahine* and Malek Khouri's (2010) *The Arab National Project in Youssef Chahine's Cinema*. As such, I did not want to write another general book about Chahine. Instead, I chose to focus on a film that exemplifies his late style: *al-Maṣīr* (The Destiny, 1997). To invent decolonial film theory, I drew on the most significant conceptual coordinates in decolonial theory, particularly as applied to aesthetics, to theorize about the exteriority of non-European cinema. To accomplish this theoretical task, extensive literature reviews of the history of Egyptian cinema and the philosophy of Ibn Rushd were required. These exemplars of Other-thought contextualize my analysis because *al-Maṣīr* must be situated within the history of Egyptian cinema, which necessitates a familiarity with this history, and also because it would be a disservice to examine *al-Maṣīr* on a purely formal level without an understanding of the film's subject (Ibn Rushd) and his philosophy. Therefore, decolonial film theory does much more than analyze a decolonial film's formal elements; it aims to methodologically center the philosophical contexts and critical histories of transmodern cinema—its pluriversal politics, liberation ethics, and decolonial aesthetics.

Throughout the book, I use the dialectical signifier "non-European" to refer to *the Other of the Other*, who lives in the exteriority of totality. Non-European is a dialectical signifier because it enacts *the negation of the negation*; in other words, it negates the negation of the non-European Other by Euromodernity. Moreover, this dialectical affirmation, through the negation of the negation, points to the *extimate* relationship between Euro-America and the tricontinent of Africa, Asia, and Latin America—a relationship marked by exterior intimacy as a result of the traumatic history of colonization.

I owe my understanding of the term "non-European" to Edward Said's (2003) illuminating essay on Sigmund Freud's non-European (Jewish) subjectivity. Said shows that Freud's ambivalence regarding his own alterity influenced his radical theorization of psychoanalysis as a discourse of Otherness, which is critical of the modern subject. To put it differently, the modern subject's self-definition depends on the nonidentity of the colonial Other. However, Freud was also a man of his time, who chose the path of Germanic assimilation in response to an ever-increasing anti-Semitic milieu, which explains his racist remarks concerning the "primitive" Other in *Totem and Taboo*, for instance.

For Said, the non-European has two meanings. Before 1945, non-European typically referred to "savage" cultures beyond European "civilization"—a case of colonial difference masquerading as cultural difference. This is the meaning Freud was working with. After 1945, and in the context of decolonization struggles throughout Africa and Asia, non-European came to signify the political possibility of a transmodern subjectivity, whose self-definition is grounded upon a sense of decolonial Otherness. As Said writes, "By 1948 the relevant non-Europeans were embodied in the indigenous Arabs of Palestine" (2003, p. 53). The transmodern subject I theorize throughout (e.g., Chahine or Ibn Rushd) is much more complex than the Cartesian modern subject because (1) the transmodern subject is reflexive about coloniality as a totalizing style of thought and (2) they choose pluralism (politics of difference) as an ethical commitment in their liberation praxis. Whereas assimilation internalizes oppression and results in sub-oppression (e.g., Freud's racism), pluralism centers dialogue in the form of intercultural translation, especially when differences are impossible to bridge. The decoloniality of both Chahine's cinema and Ibn Rushd's philosophy stems from the fact that both figures were pluralists whose works embodied ecologies of knowledges, thereby rendering them transmodern intercultural bridges between totality and exteriority.

According to Walter Mignolo and Catherine Walsh (2018), decoloniality "is the exercise of power within the colonial matrix to undermine the mechanism that keeps it in place requiring obeisance. Such a mechanism is epistemic and so *decolonial liberation implies epistemic disobedience*" (p. 114, emphasis added). My invention of decolonial film theory is a form of epistemic disobedience in the face of (colonial) film theory, and I chose to focus on the Other-thought of Chahine and Ibn Rushd because they were non-European border thinkers who embodied *ontic disobedience* by virtue of being heretics in the realms of cinema and philosophy, respectively. Their heresy was dreaming of a transmodern world characterized by cosmopolitanism *sans* colonial difference.

Non-European cinema signifies Other cinema produced in the exteriority of totality: (1) the radical films produced by Indigenous, Black, and Brown filmmakers in Euro-America and (2) the radical films produced outside of Euro-America. I say "radical" because I wish to exclude hegemonic (read: liberal and conservative) films by non-European filmmakers, which mimic the ideological cinema of Euro-America. In other words, *radical cinema enacts a critique of ideology*, which is to say it rejects oppression and affirms liberation. I will specify the contours of oppressive ideology and liberation praxis later.

Consequently, my focus here is on an example of radical Egyptian cinema, which is simultaneously part of Arab and African cinemas. Egyptian cinema can be classified, among other things, as minor or postcolonial cinema, but I choose to hone in on the decolonial dimensions of Chahine's cinema, particularly his film *al-Maṣīr*. My effort constitutes *a transmodern negation of the negation*, which is to say *a critique of the modern system's ideological totality from an exterior perspective*. This exterior perspective derives naturally from my cultural filiation with Egypt and the Arab world, but also, more importantly, from my radical affiliation with non-European peoples in general. In other words, what I negate, from an exterior perspective, is the modern system's negation of the non-European Other, which, as far as we are concerned, entails the erasure of non-European cinema and film theory. This erasure is a function of the coloniality of Euro-American cinema and film theory—one of the ideological effects of colonialism as a material structure or apparatus. I qualify my negation as transmodern because it subsumes modernity's positivity—that is, the positivity of Euro-American cinema and film theory—while affirming the exteriority of the Other. In other words, I embrace the liberatory dimensions of both Euromodernity and the historical reason of the Other. This is a radical humanist commitment, which I share with Chahine and Ibn Rushd.

As a transmodern negation of the negation, this project is a critique of the ideology of racial capitalism—an apparatus that dehumanizes, through overexploitation and other oppressive/violent means, racialized workers. The ideology of racial capitalism is the ruling-class ideology of the modern world-system, which is located in Euro-America or the Global North. Consequently, racial capitalism structures the totalizing ideology of Euro-American cinema and film theory. Conversely, this book refuses to consider non-European cinema and film theory from a modern/colonial perspective, wherein non-European cinema and film theory either do not exist or do exist but not on their own terms. Instead, I write about non-European cinema and film theory from the perspective of exteriority, which includes the border thinking of non-European peoples, such as Ibn Rushd, Quijano, Dussel, Vallega, Shafik, Fawal, Khouri, Adonis, al-Jabri, and Khatibi.

As a transmodern project, I am committed to affirming the exteriority of the non-European Other—the Other of the European Other—while subsuming modernity's positivity. This embrace of complexity, or pluriversality, in the name of liberation ethics is something that we see time and again in Chahine's cinema as well as in Ibn Rushd's philosophy, which is what attracted the former to make a film about the latter.

Some readers may wonder about my use of Latin American decolonial theory vis-à-vis Arab cinema. I am an internationalist who is committed to the Global Southern project of nonalignment, which we can reframe today in terms of alter-globalization or mundialization. As such, I have drawn on non-European thinkers from the tricontinent of Africa, Asia, and Latin America in the spirit of solidarity and comradeship. Other readers may ask why *al-Maṣīr* and not Chahine's more explicitly political film *Al Asfour* (The Sparrow, 1972)—for that I recommend Kay Dickson's (2018) "spotlight analysis" of the film. Whereas *Al Asfour* deals with the trauma of *al-naksa* (setback) in 1967, *al-Maṣīr* explores the more pressing trauma of authoritarianism, be that in the form of secular militarism or religious fundamentalism. The latter trauma continues to visibly plague the Arab world today.

To put it differently, *al-Maṣīr* provides us with a double critique of oppressive modernity and sub-oppressive antimodernity. Chahine accomplishes this double critique—a critique of totality and a self-criticism of exteriority—by prefiguring a transmodern world to come through the lens of a (non)modern world: the pluriversal politics of al-Andalus. Therefore, Chahine explodes our linear conceptions of time and progress, which are inherently modern/colonial conceptions that have been applied arbitrarily in retrospect by a variety of masters. Chahine shows us that historical reason existed before modernity, not to suggest that we should romanticize or idealize some past glory—this is *the* fascist error. Rather, with *al-Maṣīr*, Chahine is highlighting some liberatory tools for us to use today regarding important questions of politics, aesthetics, and ethics. His effort is decolonial because it rejects both oppressive coloniality and sub-oppressive (post)coloniality. In their stead, Chahine envisions a transmodern world—imagined and created from an exterior place/time—premised on cosmopolitan values such as humanism, pluralism, and democracy.

From World Cinema to Cinematic Worldliness

I begin with a critique of the term "world cinema" since this is the generic label applied to all films produced in the Global South, which in the case of this book would apply to the cinema of Egyptian filmmaker Youssef Chahine—who was known among those close to him as Joe. In other words, world cinema signifies *Other cinema* or films produced in the exteriority of Euromodernity. The label world cinema is meant to fortify the ontological equivalence between cinema and the West, or cinema *as* European, which implies an inferiority complex, cinema envy, as far as non-European cinema is concerned. The latter is either not cinema (translation: not European) or cinema-to-come (translation: not European enough). Constantin Parvulescu (2020) writes that world cinema is essentially a Eurocentric concept, which is dialectically opposed to "global cinema—that is, to Hollywood and the few other 'Woods' emulating it" (p. 53).

To put it differently, world cinema is a euphemism for third-world cinema, which is interpreted today as a derogatory term suggesting developmental deficiency not only in terms of economics but also psychologically. The third world, however, was not always considered a derogatory term, for it used to indicate tricontinental nonalignment in the context of decolonization movements from around the mid-twentieth century until the so-called end of the cold war. Therefore, the repression of the term "third" in contemporary film theory is meant to both (a) signal liberal political correctness—that is, "I'm not racist, but that is not cinema; that is world cinema"—and (b) index the waning significance of nonalignment as a Global Southern strategy of rebellion against the racial capitalist modern world-system.

While the invention of cinematic technology is undoubtedly a Euro-American innovation that can be traced to Thomas Edison and William Dickson's Kinetoscope (1891) in the United States and the Lumière brothers' Cinématographe (1895) in France, cinematic expression is a humanistic endeavor unlimited by any form of cultural particularity, ethnic or otherwise. Why then does the Egyptian film industry, which began in 1896 and has been a cinematic powerhouse in the Arab world ever since, have little to no representation in Euro-America? For me, this is not merely an academic question; it is also a personal one, for my father (Khairy) is considered one of the most influential filmmakers in the Arab world, and yet he is virtually unknown in Euro-America aside from certain niche circles. Why is that?

Josef Gugler (2011) writes, "Egypt has established one of the world's principal film industries ... Hollywood on the Nile has produced more than three thousand feature films since 1924" (p. 5), and yet Egyptian cinema "was usually regarded with condescension rather than admiration," according to Youssef Chahine, because "many people in Europe thought that all we could do was make light comedies—with belly dancing scenes, obviously—though some of us were working hard and making more worthwhile films, often on shoestring budgets" (as cited in Fargeon, 1997, p. 47).

Chahine problematizes the false universality of Euro-American cinema, which is blind to its own provinciality but projects provinciality as such onto Other cinema, such as Arab cinema: "People think that if you are not well known in the Anglo-Saxon world, you are not known at all—you're not

Introduction 7

'international.' To be international, you must show your films in Wisconsin" (as cited in Massad, 1999, p. 87). Chahine adds that the problem is systematic rather than accidental and has something to do with Orientalism—the ideology determining how Orientals (e.g., Arabs) are represented in Euro-American cinema. To Chahine, "Generally speaking, the Anglo-Saxons have trouble accepting that the Arabs have a very great civilization and that they have a very interesting past" (p. 87). This condescending attitude toward Arab culture justifies, for the Orientalist, the hegemonic negation of Arab cinema. The negation is a defense against the aesthetic self-representations of Arab filmmakers, which often embody political resistance to the cultural imperialism of Euro-American cinema. This can be contentious, for instance, when it comes to the question of Palestine because most Euro-Americans fail to see the tragic reality of the Palestinian struggle and often see the "conflict" through the ideological lens of the Israeli government.

On a side note, Chahine taught my father about film directing at the Higher Institute of Cinema in Egypt back in the 1960s, and later on, in the 1980s and 1990s, they ended up becoming competitors, particularly since both of them were always attempting to blur the line between mainstream and alternative cinema. The key number in *al-Maṣīr*, "Songs Are Still Possible," which is sung by the poet Marwan, was originally in a screenplay by my father titled *Ta'm al-Donya* (The Taste of the World). *Ta'm al-Donya* was also going to star Mohamed Mounir, the actor/singer who plays Marwan, but that film was never made. However, Chahine was not aware of this fact; rather, it was the doing of Mounir and Kawthar Mustafa. Mustafa wrote the lyrics to the song in collaboration with my father and screenwriter Yehia Azmi.

Lucia Nagib (2006) is critical of the term "world cinema," too, but she believes it is worth saving through a positive redefinition, which she provides:

> World cinema is simply the cinema of the world. It has no centre. It is not the other, but it is us. It has no beginning and no end, but is a global process. World cinema, as the world itself, is circulation … World cinema is not a discipline, but a method, a way of cutting across film history according to waves of relevant films and movements, thus creating flexible geographies … As a positive, inclusive, democratic concept, world cinema allows all

sorts of theoretical approaches, provided they are not based on the binary perspective. (p. 31)

The binary perspective is, of course, Orientalism, a discourse that divides the world hierarchically into first, second, and third on the basis of imaginary measurements of civilizational progress or psycho-economic development. I am sympathetic toward Nagib's positive redefinition, but I wish to extend her excellent analysis by proposing a new analytic term: *cinematic worldliness*. Building on Edward Said's (1983) arguments regarding "secular criticism," cinematic worldliness would indicate that films are always situated or "materially bound to their time" (p. 25); they are also "a part of the social world, human life, and of course the historical moments in which they are located and interpreted" (p. 4). Cinematic worldliness is another way of saying *transmodern cinema*, that is, radical films produced within both totality and exteriority.

In a sense, all films are local and singular, but the best films are also global and universal. What makes cinema enjoyable, in my view, depends on how successful a filmmaker is in making "a direct jump from the singular to the universal [or pluriversal], bypassing the mid-level of [cultural] particularity" (Žižek, 2000, p. 239). I believe that a filmmaker's humanistic vision—and not only their technique—facilitates this direct aesthetic jump from the singular to the pluriversal. Egyptian cinema is full of enjoyable films that are unfortunately overlooked in Euro-America, as a function of Orientalism. My attempt here is to shed light on one of these non-European films to raise the reader's critical consciousness through an expanded sense of cinematic worldliness.

This book is about the singularity of Chahine's being and the pluriversality of his cinematic thinking. It is simultaneously—as a parallel to the structure of *al-Maṣīr*—about the singularity of Ibn Rushd and the pluriversality of his philosophy. In other words, this book is not a defense of the cultural particularities of either Youssef Chahine or Ibn Rushd as non-European subjects. Of course, their identities have historical significance for their works, but they are not the main focus of my analysis.

Later on, I will define the decolonial term "pluriversality" to problematize the notion of universality, which I have no problem using as long as it does

Introduction 9

not secretly mean Euro-American universality the way cinema is a shorthand for Euro-American cinema. Cinematic worldliness, therefore, is *transmodern cinema*. The decoloniality of cinematic worldliness stems from the fact that even though it is theorized and practiced from the exteriority of—and as a delinking from the totality of—the modern system, it actually affirms and subsumes the positivity of Euro-American cinema while canceling its Orientalist negativity, be that in the form of (colonial) film theory or otherwise.

Postcolonial or Decolonial?

Before unpacking decolonial theory, I wish to address the theoretical tension between postcolonialism and decoloniality. In *Freud and Said*, I wrote:

> Walter Mignolo's (2007) distinction between postcolonialism and decoloniality is an arbitrary one premised on ethnic difference (cf. Bhambra, 2014): Afro-Asian theorists (e.g., Edward Said, Gayatri Spivak, and Homi Bhabha) v. Latin American theorists (e.g., Aníbal Quijano, Enrique Dussel, and Walter Mignolo). Here is Mignolo's (2007) statement on the key distinction between postcolonial and decolonial theorists: "The de-colonial shift, in other words, is a project of de-linking while postcolonial criticism and theory is a project of scholarly transformation within the academy" (p. 452). According to Mignolo's (2007) reasoning, Edward Said is merely a postcolonial critic albeit being a scholar-activist in every sense of the word. Said was both a Professor of English and Comparative Literature at Columbia University and a member of the Palestinian National Council.
>
> Unlike Mignolo, I am concerned with the technical or theoretical difference between postcolonialism and decoloniality, which also acknowledges the difference between postcoloniality (the neocolonial period after decolonization) and postcolonialism (the critical theorization of this period in relation to colonialism). Consequently, even though Said is typically credited for being the founder of postcolonialism, I regard him as a decolonial scholar-activist on the basis of his transmodern (Dussel, 1995) praxis of cultural resistance, or of counter-ideologically delinking colonial discourses (e.g., Orientalism) from modern fantasies of exceptionalism. (Beshara, 2021, pp. 11–12)

Ramón Grosfoguel is one of the prominent members of the Latin American modernity/coloniality research program (MCRP), which I will address in the next section. He has written critiques of postcolonialism and argued for decolonizing postcolonial studies. For example, Grosfoguel (2006) writes, "The field of postcolonial studies privileged British colonialism in India at the expense of other colonial experiences around the world" (p. 141). That may be a fair critique of the Subaltern Studies Group; however, conflating the Subaltern Studies Group with postcolonial studies as a whole is a mistake. Nevertheless, Grosfoguel's claim that the theories of Aníbal Quijano and Boaventura de Sousa Santos were ignored in "the English-centered postcolonial literature" is reasonable.

Grosfoguel adds, "Despite its many contributions to the critique of Eurocentric thinking, postcolonial studies is still a critique of Eurocentrism from the epistemic perspective of Eurocentric thinkers (Derrida, Foucault, Lacan, etc.)" (p. 142). This statement, which is directed at the postcolonial triumvirate (Spivak, Said, and Bhabha, respectively), is misleading because both Said and Bhabha have deeply engaged with the work of Frantz Fanon— who is seen as the patron saint of all things decolonial. Not to mention, of course, that Said, particularly in *Culture and Imperialism*, has drawn on the works of decolonial figures from the Global South such as Amílcar Cabral, C. L. R. James, and Walter Rodney. Furthermore, decolonial theorists can (and do) draw on European thinkers, such as Enrique Dussel's use of Emmanuel Levinas's philosophy, in their critiques of Eurocentrism.

So what does Grosfoguel (2011) mean by decolonizing postcolonial studies? On a superficial level, he suggests that we shift the focus from the South Asian Subaltern Studies Group to the Latin American Subaltern Studies Group when it comes to our critiques of Eurocentrism, given that the former group, for him, is still captivated by Eurocentric epistemology. On a deeper level, Grosfoguel is arguing that Quijano's "coloniality of power" theory provides us with the most complex description of how racial capitalism works without reducing this apparatus to the level of either culture, as postcolonial theorists do, or the political economy, as world-system analysts do.

In the end, decolonization, for Grosfoguel, is primarily epistemic, as opposed to juridico-political, which implies taking "seriously the epistemic perspectives/cosmologies/insights of critical thinkers from the Global South thinking from and with subalternized racial/ethnic/sexual spaces and bodies." According to Grosfoguel, juridico-political decolonization can lead to the establishment of a postcolonial state, but it does not result in "a radical universal decolonial anti-systemic diversality," that is, "a concrete universal … from a diversity of decolonial epistemic/ethical historical projects." While the alternative to the postcolonial state is utopian and, therefore, unclear, the dream of decolonial liberation is a worthy cause, particularly in the Global South, where neocolonialism, through economic dependence on the Global North, is the status quo.

In a less polemical style, Gurminder Bhambra (2014) attempts to stage a dialogue between postcolonialism and decoloniality while acknowledging their disciplinary/geopolitical differences: "Both postcolonialism and decoloniality are developments within the broader politics of knowledge production and both emerge out of political developments contesting the colonial world order established by European empires, albeit in relation to different time periods [nineteenth to twentieth centuries and fifteenth to twentieth centuries, respectively] and different geographical orientations [Africa/Asia and the Americas, respectively]" (p. 119). She concludes, "Postcolonialism and decoloniality are only made necessary as a consequence of the depredations of colonialism, but in their intellectual resistance to associated forms of epistemological dominance they offer more than simple opposition. They offer, in the words of María Lugones, the possibility of a new geopolitics of knowledge" (p. 120).

Furthermore, there is a distinction to be made between postcolonial film theory and decolonial film theory. While the former has been explored in numerous publications (e.g., Ponzanesi & Waller, 2012; Weaver-Hightower & Hulme, 2014), the latter has not even existed before this book, so my effort is to begin a dialogue that can be critiqued and developed by other decolonial scholars. Whereas postcolonial film theory is grounded primarily in the Other-thought of Edward Said, Gayatri Spivak, and Homi Bhabha, decolonial film theory is founded upon the border thinking of Aníbal Quijano, Enrique Dussel, and Walter Mignolo. Both theories share a radical commitment to anticolonialism as inspired by the writings of Aimé Césaire, Frantz Fanon, and C. L. R. James, among others. However, both theories use different tools to analyze colonialism.

As such, the grammar of decolonial film theory has significant contributions to make to our praxis of liberation, especially when it comes to thinking Otherwise about the dialectical relationship between the totality of modernity and the exteriority of transmodernity. Said's contrapuntal turn in *Culture and Imperialism*, for instance, aligns with the liberatory spirit of the decolonial project, for transmodernity is essentially contrapuntal—and transmodern cinema can also be framed as *contrapuntal cinema*. Therefore, there is substantial overlap between postcolonial and decolonial film theories when it comes to political practice; however, there are also crucial methodological differences as it pertains to theorizing decolonial aesthetics through the transmodern lens of liberation ethics.

Gautam Basu Thakur (2015) acknowledges the central limit of postcolonial film theory when he writes: "Postcolonial theory cannot free itself entirely from Eurocentric habits of thinking" (p. 3). Furthermore, in his book on postcolonial film theory, he applies his critical analysis to James Cameron's (2009) *Avatar*, which is the highest grossing film of all time. Decolonial film theory, conversely, decenters ideological Euro-American cinema and centers radical non-European cinema. The white savior cinematic trope deserves to be critiqued, of course, but I would rather focus on non-European subjects (authors and characters) saving themselves through delinking, border thinking, self-representation, and self-criticism.

Modernity/Coloniality

Nelson Maldonado-Torres (2008) credits W. E. B. Du Bois with implicitly announcing the decolonial turn in the early twentieth century with his identification of "the problem of the color line," but the following thinkers in particular, according to Maldonado-Torres, were (are) explicitly decolonial in their praxis: Aimé Césaire, Frantz Fanon, Gloria Anzaldúa, Lewis Gordon, Emma Perez, Chela Sandoval, Linda Tuhiwai Smith, and Boaventura de Sousa Santos. Maldonado-Torres defines the decolonial turn as

Introduction

an expression or a particular manifestation of the skepticism toward Western theodicy ... that ... finds its roots in critical responses to racism and colonialism articulated by colonial and racial subjects since the beginnings of the modern colonial experience more than five hundred years ago. (p. 7)

While the roots of decoloniality, as a counter-history, go back for centuries—being as old as the history of modern European colonialism itself—the decolonial turn "began to take definitive form after the end of the Second World War and the beginnings of the wars for liberation of many colonized countries soon after" (p. 7). In other words, *the decolonial turn marks the subjectification of the racialized object of modernity/coloniality* (i.e., the conquered, the enslaved, the damned, the oppressed), wherein a racialized subject can theorize their double-consciousness under the modern/colonial world-system. Du Bois (1903/2007), particularly in *The Souls of Black Folk*, deserves the credit bestowed upon him by Maldonado-Torres.

Today's vanguard of the decolonial turn is the Latin American modernity/ coloniality research program (MCRP). Arturo Escobar (2007) identifies the three central figures in MCRP as Aníbal Quijano, Enrique Dussel, and Walter Mignolo; however, the group includes many other thinkers I will be referring to throughout this book. The central decolonial concept is captured in the research program title: modernity/coloniality. So, what does it refer to? Escobar puts it simply: "There is no modernity without coloniality, with the latter being constitutive of the former" (p. 185). Specifically, the MCRP locates "the origins of modernity with the Conquest of America and the control of the Atlantic after 1492, rather than in the most commonly accepted landmarks such as the Enlightenment or the end of the eighteenth century" (p. 184).

The concept of modernity/coloniality can be traced back to Quijano's (2007) thesis on "the coloniality of power," which he argues "was conceived together with America and Western Europe, and with the social category of 'race' as the key element of the social classification of colonized and colonizers" (p. 171). Coloniality signifies *the ideological remainder of colonialism*, or in Quijano's words: "Eurocentered coloniality of power has proved to be longer lasting than Eurocentered colonialism" (p. 171). Quijano continues: "Coloniality of power is based upon 'racial' social classification of the world population under Eurocentered world power" (p. 171). In other words, the coloniality of power signifies racial capitalism, or that the capitalist modern world-system was always racial (and colonial) because industrial capitalism in eighteenth-century Western Europe would not have been possible without the so-called primitive accumulation of capital for hundreds of years since the colonization of the Americas in the fifteenth century.

Walter Mignolo (2007) has contributed an interesting interpretation of modernity/coloniality. For him, the *rhetoric of modernity* is sustained by the *logic of coloniality*. In my own work, I have found Mignolo's formulation useful, particularly from a psychoanalytic perspective, since it allowed me to think about *the colonial unconscious of modernity* or *how modern discourses are often ideologically founded upon colonial fantasies*. In *Decolonial Psychoanalysis* (Beshara, 2019), I analyze modernity/coloniality through Jacques Lacan's discourse of the master, and I argue that this theoretical juxtaposition provides us with a template for how ideology works.

It is worth noting here Quijano's (1993) crucial distinction between modernity and modernization. For Quijano, modernity has positive qualities, such as reason and liberation. As such, he argues that Latin America was "an active participant in the production of modernity" (p. 141). In other words, modernity, for Quijano, is not exclusively European. However, modernization entails "the transformation of the world, of society, according to the requirements of domination and control, specifically, of the domination of capital, stripped of any purpose other than accumulation" (pp. 145–6). To put it differently, modernization is "the instrumentalization of reason in the service of domination" (p. 146). This "instrumental reason" (i.e., reason + domination) is contrasted with what Quijano (p. 146) calls "historical reason" (i.e., reason + liberation). In my opinion, this decisive difference that Quijano makes between modernity and modernization is not always accounted for by the MCRP. The colonial error was conflating modernization with modernity, or instrumental reason with historical reason; unfortunately, this error continues to be repeated by many contemporary decolonial theorists.

If we accept that modernity was never exclusively European, contra the Eurocentrists, then critiquing the concept by "a decentering of modernity from its alleged European origins, including a debunking of the linear sequence linking Greece, Rome, Christianity and modern Europe" (p. 184) is warranted.

Therefore, modernity/coloniality is helpful if it specifically denotes the Eurocentric notion of modernity: modernization *qua* colonization. Rejecting oppressive modernization is necessary, but it is also crucial to articulate, from a decolonial perspective, the positive features of modernity, for they are to be subsumed by transmodernity.

Therefore, while decolonial theorists must reject instrumental reason in the name of liberation, they must also affirm historical reason. This is how I interpret the decolonial notion of delinking, developed by Samir Amin and reworked by Walter Mignolo. Delinking modernity from coloniality signifies that modernity can be liberatory and does not automatically equal oppressive modernization.

Decolonial Feminism

The previous section makes it seem like decolonial theory is a specialty of male scholars. To correct this bias, I will draw in this section on the works of decolonial feminists such as Sylvia Wynter, María Lugones, Linda Martín Alcoff, and Serene Khader. It is probably more accurate to describe Sylvia Wynter as a decolonial womanist (Paquette, 2020); having said that, Wynter (2003) extends Quijano's coloniality of power theory by addressing "the Coloniality of Being/Power/Truth/Freedom" (p. 260). She argues against Eurocentric humanism, which overrepresents Man and conflates him with an "ethnoclass (i.e., Western bourgeois) conception of the human" (p. 260). The coloniality of being, wherein European Man = human, concerns the asymmetrical power relation "between Man—overrepresented as the generic, ostensibly supracultural human—and its subjugated Human Other (i.e., Indians and Negroes)" (p. 288). Subsequently, non-Europeans, according to the coloniality of being, are rendered as not only nonhuman but also nongendered.

Furthermore, María Lugones (2010) stretches Quijano's sociological theory to address the "coloniality of gender," or how the colonized were dehumanized through the "gender system" (p. 743). She writes, "The gender system is not just hierarchical but racially differentiated, and the racial differentiation denies humanity and thus gender to the colonized" (p. 748). Lugones adds:

Gender is a colonial imposition, not just as it imposes itself on life as lived in tune with cosmologies incompatible with the modern logic of dichotomies [e.g., masculine v. feminine, human v. nonhuman, etc.], but also that inhabitations of worlds understood, constructed, and in accordance with such cosmologies animated the self-among-others in resistance from and at the extreme tension of the colonial difference. (p. 748)

For Lugones, to be a decolonial feminist means resisting the coloniality of gender: "Decolonizing gender is necessarily a praxical task. It is to enact a critique of racialized, colonial, and capitalist heterosexualist gender oppression as a lived transformation of the social" (p. 746). In other words, decolonial feminism, for Lugones, names "non-modern knowledges, relations, and values, and ecological, economic, and spiritual practices [that] are logically constituted to be at odds with a dichotomous, hierarchical, 'categorical' logic" (p. 743). Gender, as a modern/colonial concept and system, cannot account for the complexity afforded by (non)modernity as "an-other construction of the self in relation" (p. 749).

Drawing on the work of Lugones, Alcoff (2020) distinguishes between "imperial feminism" and "pluralist feminism." While the former "assumes a fixed and stable universal meaning to the idea of feminism, and does not view feminism as a dialogic, irreducibly multiple and local project" (p. 201), the latter "does not aim to achieve total coherence or consistency, and thus it must alter our vision of our political goals" (p. 210). As such, decolonial feminism—with its commitment to pluralism or multiplicity—necessitates an examination of our "non-dominant differences" or "the varied conflicts that emerge among those who are all excluded from mainstream power and status" (p. 202).

In other words, decolonial feminism affords a "multiplicity *within* worlds" or "within resistant communities, radical communities, communities of the oppressed" (p. 202, emphasis in original). Furthermore, whereas an imperial feminist may find the hierarchical binarism of the modern/colonial concept and system of gender a powerful tool, a decolonial feminist would embrace complex subjectivity in place of the coloniality of gender. After all, the objective of decolonial feminism, according to Françoise Vergès (2021), is "the destruction of racism, capitalism, and imperialism" (p. 5). These hierarchical systems of oppression reduce the world's intricacy and dehumanize the oppressed through different forms of violence: genocide, enslavement, and overexploitation.

In *Decolonizing Universalism*, Khader (2018) argues for what she calls "nonideal universalism," or a universalism that "is simultaneously feminist and anti-imperialist" (p. 21). Feminism, for Khader, is *opposition to sexist oppression*, but this opposition can be either imperialist (ethnocentric and moralist) or anti-imperialist (transnational and justice-enhancing). Consequently, she contrasts anti-imperialist feminism with what she terms "missionary feminism" or the type of ethnocentric feminism that associates "Western culture with morality" (p. 22). For Khader, the nonideal universalism of transnational feminist praxis is "about justice enhancement rather than moralist grandstanding" (p. 48).

While I will not focus in particular on the question of sex/gender in Chahine's cinema, it is fair to say that his nuanced handling of sexual difference in his films along with the ambiguity regarding his own (bi)sexuality align with the central tenet of decolonial feminism: the deconstruction of heterosexism and patriarchy, particularly as colonial legacies of Euromodernity. Furthermore, a few of Chahine's autobiographical films are currently being classified in retrospect as LGBTQ, which is a function of their pioneering representation of queer characters and their courageous exploration of homoerotic motifs, especially in *Alexandria … Why?* (*Iskandariyya … leh?*, 1979), *An Egyptian Story* (*Haddouta Misriyya*, 1982), and *Alexandria, Again and Forever* (*Iskandariyya, kaman wa kaman*, 1989).

Two Forms of Decolonization

In this section, I wish to address two forms of decolonization: material decolonization and ideological decolonization. These two forms are dialectically linked, and therefore, both are equally important. However, they are also the source of a theoretical tension between two groups of scholars who are interested in decolonization. The material decolonizers (e.g., Tuck & Yang, 2012) argue that *decolonization is not a metaphor*. Rather, for them, decolonization is literally (as in materially) unsettling. The aim of material decolonization is deoccupation, that is, undoing settler colonialism. In the context of Turtle Island, Eve Tuck and K. Wayne Yang write, "Decolonization specifically requires the repatriation of Indigenous land and life" (p. 21). This requirement is one of the central demands of the Land Back movement. Tuck and Yang add, "Decolonization eliminates settler property rights and settler sovereignty. It requires the abolition of land as property and upholds the sovereignty of Native land and people" (p. 26).

The most concrete example of material decolonization is the decolonization of Asia and Africa between 1945 and 1960 (cf. Jansen & Osterhammel, 2017; Kennedy, 2016; Shepard, 2015). However, the ideological decolonizers will argue that material decolonization without ideological decolonization results in what Kwame Nkrumah (1965) terms "neo-colonialism" as "the last stage of imperialism." Nkrumah—indexing Vladimir Lenin—wrote, "The essence of neo-colonialism is that the State which is subject to it is, in theory, independent and has all the outward trappings of international sovereignty. In reality its economic system and thus its political policy is directed from outside" (p. ix). In other words, Nkrumah is pointing to a paradoxical situation: the politico-economic dependence of postcolonial states on their former colonizers in the Global North after the end of material decolonization.

The MCRP is the current representative of ideological decolonization, and the signifier "decoloniality" is shorthand for ideological decolonization. The theoretical foundations of this camp can be traced back to the writings of Du Bois, Césaire, and Fanon, among others; however, a central text stands out in particular: Ngũgĩ wa Thiong'o's (1986) *Decolonising the Mind*. As Maldonado-Torres argues, Du Bois's (1903/2007) emphasis on "double-consciousness," this "gift of second sight," is undoubtedly a form of ideological decolonization that prefigures the decolonial turn.

Similarly, Thiong'o explores the decolonial potential of this colonized mind: an Other consciousness, which is intimately linked with an Other language and culture. Ideological decolonization is ipso facto psychic decolonization because critiquing the colonial ideology results in critical consciousness, which is another name for *a liberated consciousness, an Other way of knowing and being beyond the oppressive and violent apparatus of racial capitalism*. In sum, *postcoloniality* is material decolonization without ideological decolonization, and *decoloniality* is ideological decolonization without material decolonization. On the other hand, *liberation praxis is the dialectical process of both material (literal) and ideological (metaphorical) decolonization.*

Critiques of Decoloniality

Let us now turn to some of the major critiques of decoloniality. To begin with, Dennis Stromback (2019) attempts to bridge the theoretical gap between post-Marxism (as represented by Alain Badiou and Slavoj Žižek) and decolonial studies (as represented by Enrique Dussel), but acknowledges the impossibility of his project: "While both camps—the post-Marxists and the decolonialists—share the common struggle of fighting against the various forms of domination, the gap between them is at times difficult to overestimate" (p. 122). The impossible gap between post-Marxism and decolonial studies stems from two methodological differences: (1) the former camp's emphasis on *ontological universality* in contrast to the latter camp's prioritization of *ethical pluriversality* and (2) the former camp's *critiques of modernity from within* versus the latter camp's *critiques of modernity from without* (i.e., totality's exteriority).

The post-Marxist critique of decoloniality can be summarized as such: "Without a clear universal, grounding philosophical truth, even the decolonial critique could end up in a pyrrhic victory, as in the case of postmodern criticism becoming the new universal within the academic world" (pp. 125–6). Conversely, the decolonial critique of post-Marxism can be summed up as follows:

> The implications of a Habermasian intellectual history [i.e., that the origins of modernity are located in the Reformation, the Enlightenment, and the French Revolution] ... is that Latin America, Africa and Asia are of no importance to world history, which is nothing other than a conflation of European particularity and world universality. (pp. 128–9)

Stromback concludes, in favor of Dussel, that *transmodern pluriversality* may be the answer since it is premised on a critique of modernity from its exteriority, which affirms both reason and liberation and, therefore, avoids the ethnocentric trap of ontological universality, that is, the condensation of European particularity.

Ming Dong Gu (2020), on the other hand, is critical of decoloniality from a postcolonial perspective, for he finds the concept of decoloniality to be vague or poorly defined in the scholarly literature on the topic, particularly as articulated by Walter Mignolo:

> If decoloniality is concerned with the analysis of the underlying logic responsible for the appearance of colonialism and colonisation, how can we avoid analysing the historico-socio-economic process and conditions of colonisation? Mignolo's conception of "decoloniality" seems to have paid insufficient attention to what has brought about colonialism and coloniality in the first place. (p. 598)

In contrast to Mignolo, Gu defines decoloniality as "conditions of human existence free from coloniality, perpetrated by political, economic, social, intellectual, spiritual, and cultural decolonization" (p. 598). In other words, Gu's definition of decoloniality brings together the two forms of decolonization I previously discussed. Therefore, Gu's critique of Mignolo concerns the latter's overemphasis on ideological decolonization and his neglect of thoroughly analyzing material decolonization—a critique echoed by Joe Parker (2020) elsewhere. Gu's other reproach is that postcolonial theorists (e.g., Fanon, Said, Bhabha, Spivak) are often bracketed, or mentioned in passing, in the scholarly literature on decoloniality even though they have contributed significant writings on decolonization.

Paul Chambers (2020) takes issue with the "coloniality of knowledge" thesis, which can be traced back to the work of Peruvian sociologist Aníbal Quijano, particularly his "coloniality of power" theory. Chambers argues that "the problematic relationship between the legacy of colonialism and the production, validation and transmission of knowledge in Latin America and elsewhere is not epistemological but political and sociological" (p. 3) and that "the epistemological arguments underpinning the coloniality of knowledge thesis are problematic, especially in relation to claims made about Descartes" (p. 4).

Additionally, Chambers finds the language of decolonial theorists to be "pretentious" (p. 21). Finally, he writes: "Although decolonial thinkers are explicitly concerned about transforming social injustices, their epistemological perspective ultimately leads to relativism, which is a problematic basis for social critique and analysis" (p. 22). Similar to Gu, the focus of Chambers's criticism seems to be directed specifically at Mignolo: "Walter Mignolo is one decolonial thinker who adopts an openly relativist stance" (p. 22).

To end this section, I will now turn to a recently published book titled *Against Decolonisation: Taking African Agency Seriously*. In the book, Olúfẹ́mi Táíwò (2022) makes a conceptual distinction between two types of decolonization: *decolonization*$_1$ or "making a colony into a self-governing entity with its political and economic fortunes under its own direction," and *decolonization*$_2$ or "forcing an ex-colony to forswear, on pain of being forever under the yoke of colonisation, any and every cultural, political, intellectual, social and linguistic artefact, idea, process, institution, and practice that retains even the slightest whiff of the colonial past" (p. 3).

I find Táíwò's distinction to be similar to my discussion of the two forms of decolonization: material and ideological. Táíwò is focused on Africa in particular; as far as he is concerned, material decolonization has been achieved on the continent for the most part (save for Western Sahara) and, therefore, ideological decolonization is nothing but a "buzzword" and " a catch-all trope, often used to perform contemporary 'morality' or 'authenticity'" (p. 4).

Ultimately, Táíwò is seriously worried—and I share his concern—about decolonial scholars who reject modernity wholesale, which stems from conflating liberatory modernity with oppressive modernization, as I have previously argued. Rejecting modernity wholesale means refusing historical reason and collective liberation, which is potentially more oppressive than the colonial project of modernization since it lacks reason and entails a regressive romanticization of a fantasized bygone tradition. Fascist projects follow the authoritarian logic of this reactionary fantasy.

In contrast, Chahine's cinema is an antifascist political dream, which takes the two forms of decolonization seriously and represents them not only as aesthetic objects but also as ethical problems. This anticolonial Arabism is most visible in Chahine's film *The Sparrow* (Al Asfour, 1972), which deals with the controversial subject of *al-naksa* (setback)—the political and, more importantly, psychological defeat experienced by Arabs in 1967 after Egypt, Syria, and Jordan, in particular, lost the Six-Day War (cf. al-Azm, 2011).

The year 1967 signified the death of Arab nationalism as led by Gamal Abdel Nasser—an ambivalent figure who represented both decolonial nonalignment and (post)colonial sub-oppression. By *(post)colonial sub-oppression*, I mean the internalization of oppressive modernization by (post)colonial leaders, which often results in horizontal violence against other oppressed peoples—that is, the population they are presumably leading. As such, Nasser is credited with founding the police state in (post)colonial Egypt—clearly, his deployment of instrumental reason was for the sake of mimicking oppressive modernization as opposed to creating an authentic transmodern system, such as Arab *internationalism*. For this reason, Nasser imprisoned Egyptian communists even though he identified as a socialist. Without denying some of the liberatory dimensions of his leadership, his brand of Arab socialism *qua* nationalism was undoubtedly authoritarian and fascistic.

Chahine is a decolonial filmmaker because his radical cinema rejects both *colonial oppression* and *(post)colonial sub-oppression*. *al-Maṣīr* may not be the most obvious choice for a book on decolonial film theory; however, even though the events of the film take place in al-Andalus during the twelfth century, *al-Maṣīr* is actually a decolonial self-criticism of (post)colonial sub-oppression in Egypt, and the Arab world in general, whether this sub-oppression takes the form of secular dictatorship or Islamic fundamentalism. With *al-Maṣīr*, Chahine is exploding this alienating false choice between secular dictatorship and Islamic fundamentalism, which continues to haunt the failed politics of the contemporary Arab world.

Paradoxically, by going back in time, Chahine is prefiguring the three coordinates of a utopian Arab world to come: Arab internationalism, secular democracy, and Islamic humanism. Also, by telling a non-European story set in the Iberian Peninsula, Chahine is showing us, from a transmodern perspective, the extimate relationship between totality and exteriority. Islam is exterior to Europe, but it is not outside of it, because Islam is in a dialectical relationship with Europe—a relationship that must not be framed by Islamophobia or Islamophilia, but rather by learned ignorance vis-à-vis a forgotten (non)modern legacy of cultural exchange, particularly when we consider the influence of Ibn Rushd on European philosophy, as I will describe later on.

Furthermore, the (non)modern setting of *al-Maṣīr* is both a prenatal commentary on the birth of modernity in the fifteenth century and a postnatal exploration of transmodernity in the contemporary Arab world; therefore, the (non)modern setting of the film serves as a critique of colonial oppression and as a self-criticism of (post)colonial sub-oppression in Egypt—taken as a metaphor for the Arab world. Throughout his oeuvre, Chahine rejects both conquest from without (e.g., the French Empire, the British empire, the Ottoman Empire) and sub-oppression from within (authoritarianism and fundamentalism).

It is no coincidence that modernity begins after the negation of Judeo-Islamic alterity by Christian Spaniards, who would soon become Conquistadors negating the difference represented by the Indigenous Other the same way they negated the non-Christian/non-European Other. This rejection of difference, as the history of colonization shows, amounted to dehumanization: the negation of the Other's humanity. The forms of oppression that Chahine's liberatory cinema critiques shed light on his radical humanism, that is, his affirmation of the humanity of both the modern subject and the non-European Other, which can be alternatively phrased, from an exterior perspective, as his affirmation of the humanity of both the transmodern subject and the European Other. The latter formulation is, of course, how Chahine's characters are represented in his decolonial cinema.

Decolonial Film Theory and *al-Maṣīr*

This book is divided into two parts, preceded by an introduction and succeeded by a conclusion. In Part 1, "Decolonial Film Theory," I will unpack key decolonial concepts such as decolonial aesthesis, border epistemology, delinking, transmodernity, and pluriversality. My aim with that overview will be to sketch the contours of decolonial film theory—a "savage" methodology from the perspective of radical exteriority, which necessitates the philosophical contextualization and critical historicization of transmodern cinema. Part 2, "Decoloniality and *al-Maṣīr*," is divided into three chapters dealing with Ibn Rushd, Youssef Chahine, and *al-Maṣīr*. In the book's conclusion, I will reflect on the future of decolonial film theory.

Part 1

Decolonial Film Theory

1

Decolonial Film Theory

In the introduction, I wrote about how the (non)modern setting of *al-Maṣīr* is both a prenatal commentary on the birth of modernity in the fifteenth century and a postnatal exploration of transmodernity in the contemporary Arab-Islamic world. In other words, the (non)modern setting of the film serves as a critique of colonial oppression and as a self-criticism of (post)colonial sub-oppression. Whereas colonial oppression describes the violent techniques of administration in a settler-colony, (post)colonial sub-oppression traces the same techniques in a franchise postcolony.

The Spanish Empire's exocolonization of the Americas and the endocolonial struggle between two forms of authoritarianism—secular militarism versus Islamic fundamentalism—in Egypt are concrete examples of colonial oppression and (post)colonial sub-oppression, respectively. To further clarify these distinctions, I will discuss in some detail the differences between modernity and modernization, particularly since these ideas are dialectically explored in many of Chahine's films, including *al-Maṣīr*. Furthermore, it is vital for decolonial scholars to be able to distinguish between modernity and modernization without conflating them, which would be a grave error in any liberation praxis.

Modernity or the Instrumentalization of Reason?

Historians agree that the fifteenth century marks the beginning of the early modern period; however, the debate concerns which specific event commenced modernity. While some historians argue it was the invention of the printing press in 1440 or the Ottoman conquest of Constantinople in 1453, decolonial theorists side with those historians who associate early modernity with the European colonization of the Americas. Consequently, what are the central features of modernity aside from signifying a particular historical period with three phases (early, classical, and late)?

According to Anthony Giddens (1990), there are three major sources of the spirit of modernity: "*The separation of time and space ... The development of disembedding mechanisms ... The reflexive appropriation of knowledge*" (p. 53, emphasis in original). Giddens then identifies four institutional dimensions of modernity: industrialism, capitalism, surveillance, and military power (p. 59). While Giddens does not shy away from problematizing modernity, he defends his original position on "radicalised modernity" (pp. 149–50) against the postmodern dismissal of modernity.

The four institutional dimensions of modernity lead Alain Touraine (1995) to critique modernity when he writes, "The goal of modernity is always, and especially when it calls for the freedom of the subject, the subordination of individual interests to the interests of a whole, be it the firm, the nation, society, or reason itself" (p. 2). Just as Giddens acknowledges that modernity has both an "opportunity side" (p. 7) and a "dark side" (p. 9), Touraine unpacks the "hard" and "soft" forms of the idea of modernity to conclude that both forms have lost their "liberating and creative power" (p. 4); however, he is adamant that regressing to tradition, through nationalism or fundamentalism, is not the answer either.

Rather, Touraine is for *anti-totalitarian modernity*, conceived as "a dialogue between reason and the Subject" (p. 375). His emphasis on the importance of subjectivity in modernity is echoed in Quijano's point about the liberatory form of world modernity *qua* historical reason. Touraine writes from a theological perspective:

> Modernity destroys the sacred world, which was at once natural and divine, transparent to reason and created. It did not replace it with the world of reason and secularization ... it introduced a divorce between a *Subject* which came down from heaven to earth and was humanized, and a world of objects manipulated by *techniques*. It replaced the unity of a world created by the divine will, Reason or History, with the duality of *rationalization* and *subjectivation*. (p. 4, emphasis in original)

To Augusto Del Noce (2014), "'modernity' indicates an irreversible process of secularization" (p. 31). He adds, "In secular thought the term modernity is tied to the idea of an irreversible process toward radical immanence" (p. 76). In other words, the idea of modernity, according to Del Noce, is linked with secularization and disenchantment—as opposed to the sacred, as it is for Touraine. As we shall see next, Del Noce's view is challenged by more recent critical scholarship on modernity.

In contrast to Del Noce, Jason Josephson-Storm (2017) argues that modernity is a *"myth of a mythless society"* (p. 7, emphasis in original). For Josephson-Storm, modernity is "the sign of a rupture" and "a device for positing significant historical breaks" (p. 7); hence, why the floating signifier is polysemous. He adds: "The central feature of modernity was not the departure of the supernatural, but its uncanny persistence in the face of modernization" (p. 128).

Josephson-Storm describes modernity "not as the death of magic or the despiritualization of nature, but as the rise of mysticism and the occult" (p. 182). The myth of modernity is a narrative about the triumph of European science over (non)European religion; however, according to Josephson-Storm, this framing of "a titanic struggle between two opposing forces ... was formed in the nineteenth century; and then ... it was projected backward in a series of dramatized confrontations" (p. 13). The myth of modernity, of course, occludes instances of *science as colonial ideology* (e.g., scientific racism) and *religion as decolonial materiality* (e.g., liberation theology).

For Bruno Latour (1993),

> The word "modern" designates two sets of entirely different practices ... The first set of practices, by "translation," creates mixtures between entirely new types of beings, hybrids of nature and culture. The second, by "purification," creates two entirely distinct ontological zones: that of human beings on the one hand; that of nonhumans on the other. (pp. 10–11)

Latour's distinction parallels the decolonial division between modernity and modernization—with the latter being a reference to modernity/ coloniality specifically. But then Latour adds, "Modernity has nothing to do with the invention of humanism, with the emergence of the sciences, with the secularization of society, or with the mechanization of the world" (p. 34). For him, modernity is constituted based on numerous paradoxes of nature/society. Therefore, Latour argues that modernity "has never begun" and that there "has never been a modern world" (p. 47).

The dialectical nature of modernity was also noted by Marshal Berman (1988) when he wrote, "To be modern is to be part of a universe in which, as Marx said, 'all that is solid melts into air'" (p. 15). Latour concludes:

> If we understand modernity in terms of the official Constitution that has to make a total distinction between humans and nonhumans on the one hand and between purification and mediation on the other, then no anthropology of the modern world is possible. But if we link together in one single picture the work of purification and the work of mediation that gives it meaning, we discover, retrospectively, that we have never been truly modern. (p. 91)

According to Enrique Dussel (1995) in *The Invention of the Americas*:

> The birthdate of modernity is 1492, even though its gestation like that of the fetus, required a period of intrauterine growth. Whereas modernity gestated in the free, creative medieval European cities, it came to birth in Europe's confrontation with the Other. By controlling, conquering, and violating the Other, Europe defined itself as discoverer, conquistador, and colonizer of an alterity likewise constitutive of modernity. Europe never discovered (*descubierto*) this Other as Other but covered over (*encubierto*) the Other as part of the Same: i.e., Europe. Modernity dawned in 1492 and with it the myth of a special kind of sacrificial violence which eventually eclipsed whatever was non-European. (p. 12, emphasis in original)

In decolonial theory, 1492 is a significant date that marks a traumatic event in the history of the world: *the colonial inscription of Euromodernity through the violent and oppressive apparatus of racial capitalism*. For Dussel, the "history of world domination originates with modernity," and unlike Charles Taylor, Stephen Toulmin, and Jürgen Habermas, he does not consider modernity to be "exclusively a European occurrence" (p. 9). As such, similar to Quijano, Dussel distinguishes between modernity and modernization. In Dussel's words, "while modernity is undoubtedly a European occurrence, it also originates in a dialectical relation with non-Europe" (p. 9). In other words, Dussel differentiates between *liberatory modernity*—Quijano's historical reason—and *oppressive modernity*—a Eurocentric discourse or rhetoric of modernization that is driven by the colonial fantasies and logics of instrumental reason, whose end is the material domination of the Other.

In *Dialectic of Enlightenment*, Max Horkheimer and Theodor Adorno (1944/2002) critique the instrumental reason of the Enlightenment myth; Zygmunt Bauman (1989) goes further than them in *Modernity and the Holocaust* to argue that the Holocaust was not a failure of modernity but rather a product of modernity signifying its truth in terms of a fascistic possibility, which it contains. According to Horkheimer and Adorno, instrumental reason instrumentalizes thinking (or rationality) for control and power. In particular, instrumental reason is concerned with dominating nature, exemplified most concretely by extractive colonization. Therefore, instrumental reason tends toward fascistic ends because its oppressive logic is destructive and dehumanizing; the subhuman Other (the "savage") is equated with nature, which justifies their domination by the "civilized." Of course, this perverse way of thinking vis-à-vis the environment, or the biosphere, which has been rendered abstractly in philosophy as the subject–object problem, has led to global catastrophes from mass genocide to climate breakdown.

Oppressive modernity, in decolonial theory, is often represented as modernity/coloniality. Therefore, decolonial theorists are not critical of modernity as a whole but are specifically against oppressive modernity—or oppressive modernization, to be accurate. Dussel's term for oppressive modernity is "the myth of modernity." Additionally, the decolonial critique of modernity differs from that of the Frankfurt School critical theorists and the postmodernists. According to decolonial theorists, such as Dussel, critical modern and postmodern critiques of modernity are limited because they are critiques of modernity from within totality; therefore, they suffer from Eurocentrism. However, the decolonial critique is from without, that is, from the radical exteriority of totality, yet this critique is not a wholesale rejection of modernity, for it subsumes its positivity in the construction of transmodernity. Conversely, from the perspective of totality, the non-European Other is either negated or assimilated into the modern system.

Exteriority does not simply signify a space *outside* the totality of Euromodernity; rather, exteriority is the negation of the negation. The negation of the non-European Other along with its displacement through Orientalist images, words, and actions inform what the modern system is, for the ontological definition of totality relies structurally—albeit arbitrarily—on the negation of exteriority. To put it differently, totality and exteriority are dialectically related in the unfolding of world history, but this dialectic can only be perceived from the perspective of transmodernity because totality neutralizes difference through a politics of sameness (e.g., Christianity).

Consequently, non-European alterity is typically experienced in the oblique way the subject encounters their unconscious through dreams, slips of the tongue, symptoms, and jokes. Therefore, while the totality of the modern system has no room for the difference of the non-European Other, and may even attempt to fascistically exterminate difference altogether, the Other persists because they *ex-sist*, which signifies *the return of not only the repressed but also the oppressed*. Genocide survivors since time immemorial live to tell the tale. In other words, transmodernity accounts for this *extimate* relationship between the modern subject and the non-European Other—or the transmodern subject and the European Other—without reducing the exteriority of this Other of the Other to the totality of the modern system; transmodernity then entails a decolonial critique, as opposed to a wholesale rejection, of modernity. This decolonial critique consists of a political commitment to subsuming modernity's positivity while ethically affirming the exteriority of the Other.

Modernity's exteriority is often geographically designated as the Global South or the tricontinent of Africa, Asia, and Latin America. This geographical designation has a politico-economic implication, typically represented following what Dussel terms the "fallacy of development" or "developmentalism." For him, developmentalism signifies "the ontological position that Europe's development is assumed to be the model for every other culture" (p. 148). This Eurocentric fallacy is premised on a psychological development model, wherein so-called underdeveloped or developing cultures are positioned as children developmentally stuck at the beginning of an imaginary timeline of civilization. However, it is crucial to emphasize here that modernity's exteriority is not exclusive to the Global South, for the Global North includes reservations, ghettos, and occupied territories. Similarly, the Global South is not a utopian counter-modernity, and thereby embodies—albeit in a different way—the contradictions of global racial capitalism, such as class struggle.

Dussel defines liberatory modernity as "a world phenomenon, commencing with the *simultaneous* constitution of Spain with reference to its periphery, Amerindia, including the Caribbean, Mexico, and Peru" (p. 11, emphasis in original). In other words, Dussel's theorization of liberatory modernity can be described as both worldly and dialectical. It is *worldly* because it is not ethnocentric and *dialectical* because of its accounting of the interdependent relationship between the European center and the non-European periphery in the constitution of the modern world-system of racial capitalism. To put it differently, modernity defines itself in a dialectical (but oppressive) relationship with the exteriority it negates.

I will explore Dussel's concept of transmodernity in more detail later; it is his term for a dialectical and liberatory world modernity. As Dussel argues, Christopher Columbus did not discover the Americas; Columbus covered over the Americas. In addition to the colonial genocide of Indigenous peoples, there is also the ongoing (post)modern ethnocide of non-European peoples in the form of overwriting or covering over. The decolonial task, therefore, is to uncover this alterity, which was—and continues to be—systematically negated. The coloniality of film theory (e.g., its erasure of Other cinema) is an ideological effect of colonialism.

Coloniality is a psychic remainder of colonization. Similarly, modernity is a psychic remainder of modernization. In other words, I conceive *modernity/coloniality as the discursive-fantasmatic ideology of modernization/colonization*—another name for the ruling-class ideas of the racial capitalist apparatus. Therefore, the modern subject (i.e., the subject as such) is ipso facto a colonial subject. In Dussel's words, "The experience not only of discovery, but especially of the conquest, is *essential* to the constitution of the modern ego, not only as a subjectivity, but as subjectivity that takes itself to be the center or end of history" (p. 25, emphasis in original). Modern subjectivity is a function of colonizing Otherness. Subsequently, I wish to conceive of *transmodern subjectivity as a decolonial subjectivity that subsumes the positivity of modernity and affirms the exteriority of the Other.*

al-Maṣīr is fitting in this context because the actions of the film take place in al-Andalus, which, according to María Rosa Menocal (2002), embodied "a complex culture of tolerance" (p. 36) for around eight centuries. al-Andalus is a concrete example of transmodernity, for that signifier challenges ethnocentric accounts of European geography and history. Dussel (2013) classifies that period as the third stage of the interregional system—an Afro-Asiatic and Mediterranean system with the Muslim world as its center alongside China, Bantu Africa, and the Byzantine-Russian world. The Muslim world went from being at the center of the third interregional system in the seventh century to being at the periphery of the Euromodern world-system since the fifteenth century.

al-Andalus indexes a time/place wherein alterity was sublated dialectically through historical reason. Muslims ruled a significant portion of the Iberian Peninsula for 781 years, yet Islam and Muslims are routinely excluded from the European popular imagination since they signify an Oriental Otherness that must be kept at bay, if not dominated (cf. Said, 1978/2003). Hence, we face a theoretical tension between (1) a material and worldly history, which accounts for cultural complexity, and (2) an ideological and ethnocentric story written by the so-called victors and echoed by the paranoid "clash of civilizations" myth.

It is no coincidence that the Americas were colonized in the same year that Muslims and Jews were expelled from Spain after the fall of Granada. In *Decolonial Psychoanalysis* (Beshara, 2019), I also show how the Spanish Conquistadors perceived Amerindians through the lens of their religious racism vis-à-vis Muslims and Jews. In other words, oppressive modernity was instituted precisely to exclude non-Christian/non-European alterity. Over time, the criteria of exclusion that determined "civilized" and "savage" were expanded based on biology and culture. The theologically justified racism— cf. Valladolid debate (1550–1)—became scientifically and legally justified over the years, particularly since the hegemonic rise of social Darwinism during the nineteenth century.

The major premise in the myth of modernity, according to Dussel (1995), is Eurocentrism; that is, the myth that "Europe is more developed" and that "its civilization is superior to others" (p. 66). The logical consequence of the Eurocentric premise is the civilizing mission, wherein the "primitive"/"barbarian" (i.e., "savage") Other must be "civilized" through domination: extermination or assimilation. If the assimilated Other is not enslaved, he or she is rendered a second-class citizen.

The civilizing mission is a concrete example of the workings of modernization and its oppressive utilization of instrumental reason. Bauman (1989) defines the civilizing process as "*a process of divesting the use and deployment of violence from moral calculus, and of emancipating the desiderata of rationality from interference of ethical norms or moral inhibitions*" (p. 28, emphasis in original). This same modern/colonial logic informs the power dynamics existing in the Euro-American film world today, which continues to marginalize non-European cinema and film theory. Border filmmakers and decolonial film theorists are given an alienating false choice: assimilate or evaporate. To get a better understanding of these modern/colonial power dynamics, I must first unpack some central concepts in decolonial theory regarding the coloniality of power/knowledge/being.

Coloniality of Power, Knowledge, and Being

Coloniality of Power

Peruvian sociologist Aníbal Quijano was the first to posit the "coloniality of power" theory, which is almost identical to the concept of racial capitalism developed by a brilliant group of Black Marxists: Cedric J. Robinson, Robin D. G. Kelley, and Ruth Wilson Gilmore. For Quijano (2000), the coloniality of power signifies a matrix of domination structured on two axes: the racial and labor axes. In Quijano's words:

> America was constituted as the first space/time of a new model of power of global vocation, and both in this way and by it became the first identity of modernity. Two historical processes associated in the production of that space/time converged and established the two fundamental axes of the new model of power. One was the codification of the differences between

conquerors and conquered in the idea of "race," a supposedly different biological structure that placed some in a natural situation of inferiority to the others. The conquistadors assumed this idea as the constitutive, founding element of the relations of domination that the conquest imposed. On this basis, the population of America, and later the world, was classified within the new model of power. The other process was the constitution of a new structure of control of labor and its resources and products. This new structure was an articulation of all historically known previous structures of control of labor, slavery, serfdom, small independent commodity production and reciprocity, together around and upon the basis of capital and the world market. (pp. 533–4)

In addition to defining the coloniality of power, Quijano (2007) was also keen to distinguish coloniality from colonialism: "Coloniality, then, is still the most general form of domination in the world today, once colonialism as an explicit political order was destroyed" (p. 170). I have described *coloniality as the psychic remainder of colonialism*, but it can also be characterized, following Said (1978/2003), as a "style of thought based upon an ontological and epistemological distinction made between 'the Orient' and (most of the time) 'the Occident'" (p. 2).

Mignolo (2007) refers to coloniality as the "logic" of modernity; he frames the latter as "rhetoric." I have extended Mignolo's distinction in *Decolonial Psychoanalysis* by theorizing modernity as a discourse sustained by a colonial fantasy; as such, I was able to conceive of modernity/coloniality as an ideology following Žižek. In *Freud and Said* (Beshara, 2021), I further stretched my analysis by grounding the ideology of modernity/coloniality in the material apparatus of global racial capitalism. Concretely, the coloniality of power is a hierarchical matrix of domination that structures human difference based on race and class.

The sexual axis is certainly of import, too, as demonstrated by María Lugones (2010) with her theorization of the "coloniality of gender." In my work, I have addressed the coloniality of gender through the Lacanian psychoanalytic theorization of sexual difference, which I argue structures the zone of being—a zone occupied mainly by bourgeois Euro-Americans. Whereas the "zone of nonbeing"—Frantz Fanon's (1952/2008) name for the zone occupied by the damned of the Earth—is structured by colonial difference. Other decolonial theorists, primarily Mignolo, have written about colonial difference, but I may have been the first to explore the concept from a psychoanalytic perspective; in other words, *coloniality is the unconscious of modernity*.

If I were to place coloniality on a historical trajectory, I would write: premodern conquest (fourth millennium BCE to fifteenth century CE) → modern colonialism (fifteenth century CE to present) → postmodern coloniality (1945–present). Modern colonialism overlaps with postmodern coloniality because, while it is no longer an "explicit political order" in many parts of the world, it continues to exist as a material structure; therefore, we should not regard colonialism as merely a historical event. However, we can confidently assert that a paradigm shift occurred in the fifteenth century when the modern world-system of racial capitalism replaced the interregional systems that preceded it.

So, while the Arabs did conquer the Iberian Peninsula in the eighth century, their model of power is distinguishable from the coloniality of power to emerge centuries later with the advent of modern colonialism. According to historian Adnan Husain (2022), "All pre-modern empires conquered territory, which is distinguished from colonialism by a nation-state dominating and exploiting another nation or people and their territory" (personal communication). In other words, while the Arabs did conquer territory in the Iberian Peninsula, later designated as al-Andalus, they did not dominate and exploit the peoples of that land—be they Christians or Jews—following the coloniality of power model—cf. the myth of the "Arab invasion" (Lacoste, 1984).

Furthermore, Robert Hoyland (2020) argues:

> Because the homeland of the Europeans was so far away from their colonies and because fewer Europeans relocated to them, the culture of the Europeans was relatively little affected by that of those they conquered; mostly the influence was one way, with the Europeans inflicting substantial changes upon the indigenous cultures that they ruled. In the Muslim Arab case the influence was two-way, with the conquered population participating in a very substantial way in the new Islamic civilization that emerged in the wake of the Muslim Arab conquests. (p. 26)

So, what is colonialism? Ronald Horvath's (1972) attempt at defining colonialism has been influential in scholarly literature. For him, it is a form of domination—"the control by individuals or groups over the territory and/or behavior of other individuals or groups" (p. 46)—and a form of exploitation. He also distinguishes between colonialism and imperialism based on "the presence or absence of significant numbers of permanent settlers in the colony from the colonizing power" (p. 47).

For Said (1993), the distinction follows a similar logic: "'Imperialism' means the practice, the theory, and the attitudes of a dominating metropolitan center ruling a distant territory; 'colonialism,' which is almost always a consequence of imperialism, is the implanting of settlements on distant territory" (p. 9). This settlement question is important regarding the two main typologies of colonialism: franchise colonialism and settler colonialism. For example, Egypt was a British franchise colony exploited from afar—the Euromodern metropole of London. The United States, on the other hand—or Israel, for that matter—is a settler colony par excellence, wherein European settlers displaced the Indigenous peoples who ruled this land for thousands of years.

Whiteness, as an ideology or "as a ruling-class social control formation" (Allen, 2012, p. 322), was invented in the United States in the seventeenth century, in the context of Bacon's Rebellion (1676–7), to establish solidarity among European settlers, regardless of their class interests, particularly against the racialized. According to Theodore Allen (2012), the "white race" was invented "as the solution to the problem of social control" (p. 47). Furthermore, Allen shows how the "Act concerning Servants and Slaves" "formally instituted the system of privileges for European-Americans, of even the lowest social status, *vis-à-vis* any person of any degree of African ancestry, not only bond-laborers but free Negroes as well" (p. 47, emphasis in original).

The historical function of whiteness in the coloniality of power supports Quijano's assertion regarding the racial axis. In other words, racism has been baked into capitalism since its early beginnings in so-called primitive accumulation. It is no coincidence that Quijano presents the racial axis before the labor axis. The colonizers debated who was human and who was not before addressing the commodity question and its fetishization. Those who were considered nonhuman by the colonizers were, of course, enslaved and rendered as fungible commodities to be overexploited.

Coloniality of Knowledge

Michel Foucault (1980) is perhaps the most popular theorist who wrote about the interdependence of power and knowledge through his concept of power/knowledge (*pouvoir-savoir*): "Once knowledge can be analysed in terms of region, domain, implantation, displacement, transposition, one is able to capture the process by which knowledge functions as a form of power and disseminates the effects of power" (p. 69). However, he did not analyze that relationship in terms of coloniality, which is what Quijano (2000) did when he described the coloniality of knowledge as "a mental operation" that made Europeans "feel not only superior to all the other peoples of the world, but, in particular, *naturally superior*" (p. 541, emphasis added).

The coloniality of knowledge "generated a new temporal perspective of history and relocated the colonized population, along with their respective histories and cultures, in the past of a historical trajectory whose culmination was Europe" (p. 541). In other words, the coloniality of knowledge made possible the framing of non-Europeans as "inferior races" (p. 542) or "savages." The coloniality of knowledge produces a "binary, dualist perspective on knowledge" (p. 542), which can be described as Eurocentric and Orientalist.

The framework of Orientalism works here because even though the Americas were west of Europe, the Conquistadors categorized the Indigenous peoples of the Americas as "Indians" since they intended to sail to the Orient (India) through the Atlantic Ocean. Furthermore, as I have mentioned earlier, the Conquistadors perceived the Indigenous peoples of the Americas through their schematic encounters with non-Christian/non-European Others, namely Muslims and Jews. This explains why the US military, in the twenty-first century, used the code name "Geronimo" to refer to Osama bin Laden. Eurocentrism and Orientalism are colonial epistemic operations meant to police the boundaries of Europeanness (and, later, whiteness) *qua* civilized humanity.

The coloniality of knowledge imagines

> modernity and rationality as exclusively European products and experiences. From this point of view, intersubjective and cultural relations between Western Europe and the rest of the world were codified in a strong play of new categories: East-West, primitive-civilized, magic/mythic-scientific, irrational-rational, traditional-modern—Europe and not Europe. (p. 542)

Therefore, we can think of *the epistemic negation of non-European ways of knowing as the colonial unconscious of Euromodernity,* for, as Quijano shows, the colonizers "repressed as much as possible the colonized forms of knowledge production, the models of the production of meaning, their symbolic universe, the model of expression and of objectification and subjectivity" (p. 541). Eurocentrism, as the dominant form in the coloniality of knowledge, "began in Western Europe before the middle of the seventeenth century, although some of its roots are, without doubt, much older" (p. 549). Quijano adds that the constitution of Eurocentrism "was associated with the specific bourgeois secularization of European thought and with the experiences and necessities of the global model of capitalist (colonial/modern) and Eurocentered power established since the colonization of America" (p. 549).

Quijano then outlines the three central elements of Eurocentrism in the coloniality of knowledge:

> (*a*) a peculiar articulation between dualism (capital–precapital, Europe–non-Europe, primitive–civilized, traditional–modern, etc.) and a linear, one-directional evolutionism from some state of nature to modern European society; (*b*) the naturalization of the cultural differences between human groups by means of their codification with the idea of race; and (*c*) the distorted-temporal relocation of all those differences by relocating non-Europeans in the past. (pp. 552–3, emphasis in original)

As a function of the coloniality of knowledge, non-European theorists often do more intellectual labor than their European counterparts, for they have to study the knowledge produced in their cultural traditions alongside European epistemology, which is what Ibn Rushd did in his synthesis of Aristotelianism and Islam, for instance. For the most part, European theorists exclusively study their intellectual production and often assume it to be inherently superior. And when they study the Orient, as Said (1978/2003) shows, they do so through the distorting lens of Eurocentrism. This is not to suggest that there is a direct way to knowledge; however, Other intellectual traditions are to be wrestled with and cannot simply be dismissed. Ultimately, self-representation through learned ignorance is the decolonial path of least resistance.

In the next chapter, I will be discussing in depth Ibn Rushd and his philosophy. Ibn Rushd exemplifies the double work of transmodernity, for he was a Muslim jurist well versed in the Islamic tradition and also an expert on Aristotelian philosophy. This double work results from the double-consciousness that non-European subjects embody, as documented by Du Bois concerning African Americans. Now, Ibn Rushd was living in a different context, of course, before the advent of modern colonialism. Consequently, pluriversality was more effortless to realize before the colonial hegemony of Eurocentric knowledge.

Now, I must turn to René Descartes since he is considered one of the founders of modern European philosophy. Our current ideas about modern subjectivity (*ego cogito*) stem largely from Cartesian philosophy; Dussel (1995) argues that the *ego cogito* of seventeenth-century Europe would not have been possible without its foundation in the *ego conquiro* of the fifteenth century. In his words, "The 'I-conquistador' forms the protohistory of Cartesian *ego cogito* and constitutes its own subjectivity as will-to-power" (p. 43, emphasis in original).

According to Descartes, the thinker, who is the basis for being, is not any thinker/being in the world but a specific Euromodern thinker/being who would not have existed if it were not for the colonization of the Americas and the primitive accumulation of capital through extraction, genocide, enslavement, and overexploitation. Consequently, the Cartesian categorization excludes non-European thinkers/beings who are essentially negated, that is, rendered nonthinking/nonbeing.

For this reason, Eurocentrists continue to distinguish between European *philosophy* and non-European *thought*, which implies that the latter is not rigorous or systematic enough to be considered philosophy. Non-European thought is a code for religion or culture but not philosophy. Therefore, even when the word "thought" refers to systematic non-European knowledge, it does not have the same weight as Cartesian thinking—a type of rationality (i.e., instrumental reason) that is exclusively European.

Ramón Grosfoguel (2013) extends Dussel's thesis by asserting, "What links the 'I conquer, therefore I am' (*ego conquiro*) with the idolatric, God-like 'I think, therefore I am' (*ego cogito*) is the epistemic racism/sexism produced from the 'I exterminate, therefore I am' (*ego extermino*)" (p. 77, emphasis in original). Grosfoguel locates the *ego extermino* in the long sixteenth century and documents four genocides/epistemicides that this ego was responsible for:

1) against Muslims and Jews in the conquest of Al-Andalus in the name of "purity of blood"; 2) against indigenous peoples first in the Americas and then in Asia; 3) against African people with the captive trade and their enslavement in the Americas; 4) against women who practiced and transmitted Indo-European knowledge in Europe [and who were] burned alive [and] accused of being witches. (p. 77)

I have previously indexed Quijano's distinction between instrumental reason and historical reason. I will say more about historical reason in the section on the decoloniality of knowledge, but I wish to end this section with some words on instrumental reason. The coloniality of power/knowledge instrumentalizes (un)reason for the sake of domination, which is the fascistic horizon of modernization. According to Quijano (1989):

The world dominance of the "Anglo-Scottish" version of modernity, that of instrumental reason, was strengthened and extended when British imperial hegemony gave way to North American hegemony at the end of the Second World War. The Pax Americana established after the defeat of Nazism, and the further weakening of historical reason during that period, exacerbated both the characteristics and the consequences of the domination of instrumental reason. (p. 154)

If instrumental reason is the means, then fascistic modernization is the end—bearing in mind Bauman's point about the Holocaust being a possibility within modernity as opposed to an accident. However, what is the promise of this fascistic modernization? For Quijano, to modernize means to accept a rationality shorn of all connections with the original promises of modernity, a rationality now totally and solely possessed by demands of capital and productivity, by the efficiency of the means to secure the ends imposed by capital and by empire—in the last analysis, reason as the mere instrument of power. (p. 154)

Coloniality of Being

In *Black Skin, White Masks*, Frantz Fanon (1952/2008) was the first theorist to write explicitly about the coloniality of being, "There is a zone of nonbeing, an extraordinarily sterile and arid region, an incline stripped bare of every essential from which a genuine departure can emerge" (p. 22). Fanon was writing about the dehumanization of Black men specifically in the context of coloniality (psychic colonization), but we can extend his analysis to racialized subjects in general.

However, it is important to acknowledge the specificity of anti-Black racism in constructing a white supremacist world, and Maldonado-Torres (2007) acknowledges this when he says, "The enigma of blackness appears as the very radical starting point to think about the coloniality of Being" (p. 253). Similarly, Tommy Curry (2017) writes, "The Man-Not is a theoretical formulation that attempts to capture the reality of Black maleness in an anti-Black world" (p. 7). Curry uncovers the perverse racial-sexual nature of anti-Black misandry and how it is ultimately geared toward genocidal ends as far as Black males are concerned—since they are the subordinate male targets of white supremacist violence/oppression within the apparatus of racial capitalism. The specificity of anti-Black racism is a function of the metaphor of dirt used by racist colonizers (Kovel, 1970). Incidentally, as Daniel José Gaztambide (2019) shows, Jews were perceived as Black—or, at least, as nonwhite—by Nazis, which folds anti-Semitism into anti-Black racism.

Maldonado-Torres (2007) is the contemporary theorist of the coloniality of being; however, he credits Mignolo for coming up with the concept in the mid-1990s. Maldonado-Torres writes, "While the coloniality of power referred to the interrelation among modern forms of exploitation and domination (power), and the coloniality of knowledge had to do with [the] impact of colonization on the different areas of knowledge production, coloniality of being would make primary reference to the lived experience of colonization and its impact on language" (p. 242).

Following this definition, *Decolonial Psychoanalysis* examined the coloniality of being a US Muslim in the context of the "war on terror" discourse and the Islamophobia/Islamophilia fantasy—a politicized context, of course, which positions US Muslims as guilty until proven innocent. I documented qualitatively, through Lacanian discourse analysis, two subject-positions US Muslims adopt to resist Islamophobia through either critical knowledge or their very being (Beshara, 2019). After all, to exist is to resist, which is the motto of the Palestinian praxis of *sumud* (steadfastness).

Maldonado-Torres understands the coloniality of being in terms of the *ego conquiro*, which is the foundation of the *ego cogito*. In other words, the modern ontological positing of *being* presupposes a nonbeing exterior to modernity (i.e., the "barbarian"); similarly, the modern epistemological emphasis on *thinking* implies a nonthinking subject before modernity (i.e., the "primitive"). Following the coloniality of being, Chahine would be positioned—albeit unconsciously—as a "barbaric" filmmaker who made a "savage" film about a "primitive" philosopher (Ibn Rushd). For Maldonado-Torres, the coloniality of being is essentially a Fanonian challenge to both Descartes and Heidegger from the perspectives of the damned of the Earth, who were excluded from Euromodern theorizations of subjectivity.

Maldonado-Torres writes, "The *damné* is for the coloniality of Being what Dasein is for fundamental ontology, but, as it were, in reverse. The *Damné* is for European Dasein the being who is 'not there'" (p. 253, emphasis in original). Therefore, the coloniality of being accounts for the processes of ontological colonial difference under racial capitalism, wherein civilizational discourses are often invoked to distinguish between who is "civilized" and who is "savage," that is, who is human and who is nonhuman. In sum, who are the (non)beings, and what are the (non)thoughts, negated by Euromodernity? This book enacts an answer to these questions through a decolonial analysis of Chahine's cosmopolitan being and border thinking as embodied in the radical exteriority of his transmodern cinema. In order to do that, I must now shift to unpacking some other decolonial concepts.

Delinking and Border Thinking

Mignolo (2007) invokes Samir Amin's notion of delinking and connects it with Quijano's "project of 'desprendimiento'" (p. 452). For Mignolo, delinking (or *desprenderse*) is a decolonial epistemic methodology, which is meant to enact a shift toward liberation: *"pluriversality as a universal project"* (pp. 452–3, emphasis in original). Mignolo writes, "Delinking in my argument presupposes border thinking or border epistemology in the precise sense that the Western foundation of modernity and of knowledge is on the one hand unavoidable and on the other highly limited and dangerous" (p. 455).

Border thinking, as an epistemology, is inspired by the work of Gloria Anzaldúa. Mignolo (2012) acknowledges Anzaldúa in his new preface to *Local Histories/Global Designs*:

> The body-politics of knowing, thinking, and doing comes from bodies who dwell and think in the borders. For millions of people around the world who dwell in the border, Anzaldúa provided a way of thinking that incorporates experiences not previously reflected (except, perhaps, partially and indirectly) in even the most superb and magnificent expressions of European thoughts. (p. xx)

Mignolo (2007) stresses that delinking

> means to change the terms of the conversation, and above all, of the hegemonic ideas of what knowledge and understanding are and, consequently, what economy and politics, ethics and philosophy, technology and the organization of society are and should be, it is necessary to fracture the hegemony of knowledge and understanding that have been ruled, since the fifteenth century and through the modern/colonial world by what I conceive here as the theo-logical and the ego-logical politics of knowledge and understanding. (p. 459)

To put it differently, delinking is not about throwing the baby (modernity) out with the bathwater (coloniality). Rather, it is about delinking the *logic* of coloniality from the *rhetoric* of modernity, which constitutes a new decolonial grammar (e.g., decolonial film theory) that questions the false universality of Euromodern theories and practices and proposes pluriversal politics in their stead. Delinking, therefore, involves an epistemic shift from *the universality of theo-/ego-politics* to *the pluriversality of geo-/body-politics*.

Mignolo writes that "one strategy of de-linking is to de-naturalize concepts and conceptual fields that totalize A reality" (p. 459); this strategy is typically enacted from the perspective of radical exteriority. It is worth noting that Chahine was a border thinker, particularly if we consider Alexandria as a border city between North Africa and Europe. As a border filmmaker, Chahine aesthetically delinked coloniality from modernity through his transmodern cinema, which he did through both his unique style and his solidarity with the oppressed. This solidarity took the shape of an anticolonial and antiauthoritarian politics of *iltizām* (commitment), which championed historical reason; Chahine's radical politics was embodied both in his personal life and in the subject matters of his films.

While I have learned a great deal from Mignolo, I have two major critiques of his work:

(1) Delinking coloniality from modernity ought to mean sublating the best of modernity as opposed to rejecting modernity wholesale. The sublating dimension of delinking is present in Dussel's writings, but it is absent in Mignolo's account, as evidenced by his anti-Marxism. Third World Marxism, which must be critiqued, has unquestionably been a necessary force in the decolonization of many nation-states in the Global South and the formation of the Non-Aligned Movement in the context of the cold war between the United States and the Soviet Union.

(2) There is a distinction between critiquing postcolonialism and harshly criticizing the field using false claims to make a strong case for decoloniality as the better theoretico-practical alternative. In truth, there is a lot in common between postcolonialism and decoloniality that the situation can be characterized psychoanalytically, following Freud, as the narcissism of minor differences. Mignolo falsely claims, "post-colonial criticism and theory is a project of scholarly transformation within the academy" (p. 452). This claim is incorrect for several reasons, the most significant of which is that Said's work, for instance, as a member of

the Palestinian National Council, is unmatched by any self-identifying decolonial theorist living or dead.

I mention Said, in particular, because he is considered to be one of the founders—if not *the* founder—of postcolonial studies. In his attack on postcolonialism, Mignolo places Said up against the wall alongside the usual suspects (Spivak and Bhabha). In other words, a decolonial firing squad of the metaphorical variety is counterproductive, in my view, when Marxist and postcolonial comrades are indispensable in our delinking projects from colonialism and coloniality.

The Egyptian social theorist Samir Amin, from whom Mignolo draws, is an example of a decolonial (Third World) Marxist to whom we ought to turn now. In his book, Amin (1990) puts forth four propositions on the necessity of delinking from global (racial) capitalism as a modern world-system:

> First, the necessity of delinking is the logical political outcome of the unequal character of the development of capitalism … Second, delinking is a necessary condition of any socialist advance, in the North and in the South … Third, the potential advances that become available through delinking will not "guarantee" certainty of further evolution towards a pre-defined "socialism" … Fourth, the option for delinking must be discussed in political terms. (p. xiv)

For Amin, "Delinking is not synonymous with autocentric development. It indicates another phenomenon: a demand imposed by the system. It is the condition for autocentric development, on the basis of a legacy of peripheral capitalism" (p. 18). Amin, therefore, is interested in delinking "the criteria of rationality of internal economic choices from those governing the world system" (pp. 18–19). In other words, Amin is considering the (im)possibility of nation-states in the Global South delinking materially, or politico-economically, from the Global Northern apparatus of racial capitalism. Consequently, for Amin, the horizon delinking points to is socialism. I would even qualify his vision as not only socialist but also antiracist since he was writing from the periphery (Senegal) about a polycentric world—another term for pluriversality.

As I have mentioned before, border thinking is inspired by the work of Anzaldúa, particularly her 1987 book, *Borderlands/La Frontera*, in which she writes about "border culture" as a "third country" (p. 3). To Mignolo (2012), "it is the recognition of the colonial difference from subaltern perspectives that demands border thinking" (p. 6). Mignolo defines border thinking as "the moments in which the imaginary of the modern world system cracks" (p. 23), for it is an Other way of thinking beyond the images and the imaginations of Euromodern intellectuals who often consider neither the colonial logics of their rhetoric nor the material and ideological effects of these colonial logics.

I understand *border thinking as thinking critically from the radical exteriority of Euromodernity* (i.e., beyond its borders). These borders are both literal and metaphorical. Literally, they are traumatic sites where refugee crises originating in the Global South are often most visible; these sites raise the question of *ontological colonial difference*. Judith Butler (2016) has addressed this question of ontological colonial difference through what she terms the politics of grievability: when is life grievable? Non-European victims, for example, are rarely considered grievable in Euro-America media.

Metaphorically, borders signify the intellectual disciplining of knowledge, that is, what or who is worth knowing? *Epistemic colonial difference* is enacted, for example, in the distinction between (European) *philosophy* and (non-European) *thought*. Said (1978/2003) provided us, in *Orientalism*, with one of the most rigorous studies of epistemic colonial difference through his meticulous analysis of Euromodern representations of the Orient, which follow the structure of dreams.

In other words, even though Orientalist texts say more about Orientalists (and their desires) than they do about the Orient, these texts are nevertheless posited as repositories of knowledge about the Orient—that "dark" tricontinent. If we accept the decolonial thesis that a colonial logic unconsciously undergirds any modern rhetoric, negating non-European alterity then is never accidental but always intentional. Subsequently, in terms of the geo-/body-politics of being and knowing, we can say that Chahine was frequently implementing a border epistemology in his exterior filmography, which indexed ideas, places, and peoples often negated by the rhetoric of Euromodernity. In other words, there is a decolonial logic at work throughout Chahine's oeuvre, which is expressed manifestly in a transmodern rhetoric: the aesthetic form of his radical cinema.

Transmodernity and the Ethics of Liberation

Enrique Dussel came up with the concept of transmodernity as an alternative to both critical modernity and postmodernity since both approaches are ultimately critiques of modernity from within totality. *Critical modernity* is best represented by the critical theory of the Frankfurt School, which never included non-European ontologies, epistemologies, or methodologies in its critiques of Euromodernity. *Postmodernity* is seen as throwing the baby (modernity) out with the bathwater (coloniality), which amounts to not only a critique of instrumental reason but also, more dangerously, a wholesale rejection of reason.

Transmodernity, on the other hand, is a critique of modernity from its radical exteriority; it is a dialectical—although Dussel prefers the term *analectical*—critique, which sublates modernity *sans* coloniality through the historical reasoning of the non-European Other. As such, transmodernity is both *a rejection of instrumental (or colonial) reason* and *an affirmation of historical (or decolonial) reason*. Historical reason becomes decolonial reason through "an amplified rationality which makes room for the reason of the Other" (Dussel, 1995, p. 131). In other words, there is no collective liberation without historical reason.

In *The Invention of the Americas*, Dussel (1995) describes transmodernity as "a project of the future" (p. 12), for it is indeed a utopian horizon "characterized by ecological civilization, popular democracy, and economic justice" (p. 117). In the praxis of liberation, "*transmodern worldhood*" entails affirming "the reason of the Other" (p. 26, emphasis in original). For Dussel, transmodernity then "upholds negated alterity, the dignity and identity of the other cultures, and the covered-over (*en-cubierto*) Other" (p. 66, emphasis in original).

Chahine embodied a decolonial subjectivity, and his films showcased transmodern worlds, for he valued both Euromodern and non-European ways of being and knowing. Chahine was extremely proud of his Egyptian heritage but was also unashamedly a Francophone. The alienating choice between Euromodernity and its non-European alterity is ultimately a false choice. Chahine poetically addressed the colonial logic of this alienation in his 2011 interview with documentary filmmaker Mark Cousins: "We've proven that we were civilized seven thousand years ago. Are we so underdeveloped? That's not civilization. Civilization is how to contact the other people. Do you know how to love? Do you know how to care? This is civilization." As such, transmodernity involves traversing colonial fantasies through a dialogical affirmation of the best of modernity and its alterity. As is clear from Chahine's answer, this traversal is ethical, hence the centrality of ethics in liberation praxis. The question of liberation ethics is how we collectively determine what we consider to be good or just, which has to do with what and how we desire and enjoy as comrades.

Dussel (2013) takes up this precise question of the good or the just in his magnum opus *Ethics of Liberation*, wherein he surveys all the major theories of ethics, modern and otherwise, to imagine "an ethics of the body and its reality and an ethics of life" (p. 50) beyond all forms of ethnocentrism. Dussel grounds this pluriversal ethics materially in terms of "the demand (or obligation) of the production, reproduction, and development of the life of the human subject" (p. 478). While the "ethics of liberation is a possible ethics regarding any action of everyday life" (p. 373), the privileged ethical subject of liberation praxis "is the victim or community of victims" (p. 374). It is impossible to summarize Dussel's sophisticated account here, but suffice it to say that, in his system, ethics is more foundational than ontology. As we shall see later in the book, Chahine's transmodern cinema also privileges ethics over ontology through *an ethics of care for the Other.*

Dussel's ethics of liberation is in line with Paulo Freire's (1970) thesis regarding the leadership of the oppressed, which, as praxis of liberation, provides us with an alternative to the revolutionary model. In revolution, the oppressed—that is, the proletariat or their representatives in the form of a vanguard party—replace the oppressors in the hierarchy of power to form the central committee. As history shows, the "democratic" centralism of said central committee is, in practice, an authoritarian mirage.

Liberation praxis, on the other hand, is an ethical process that actualizes a nonhierarchical (or libertarian) model of power. The signifier "leadership" designates an avant-garde position on the horizon as opposed to the vertical dominance of a vanguard party. However, this leadership must be democratically legitimated by the oppressed to avoid tragic scenarios of sub-oppression, wherein the oppressed are repeating older dynamics used against them through the use of horizontal violence. In liberation praxis, the goal is the humanization of all—including the oppressors. Nevertheless, the oppressors cannot lead since, when they had the semblance of power (i.e., violence), they used it to dehumanize the Other. This principle of liberation applies regarding the hegemony of Euro-American cinema and film theory, too, which must also take a back seat.

Consequently, the liberatory task, when it comes to *decolonial aesthetics* (cf. Ramos, 2018), is listening ethically to the voices of non-European artists, which can be a challenge for Europeans—given the problem of "false generosity" identified by Freire (1970, p. 44). Chahine was triggered—in the response I cited above—by Cousins, who probably referred to him as a "Third World filmmaker." Chahine refused the hierarchical—and colonial—designation not only for what it implies in terms of his transmodern subjectivity (a third-rate filmmaker?) but also for how it denigrates Egyptian culture. Chahine tells Cousins, "I am the Third World? No, you are!" Chahine's transmodern subjectivity was characterized by a *singularity of being and a pluriversality of thinking*. These characteristics are most visible in his autobiographical films, wherein he used the traumatic experiences of his life but elevated them to an enjoyable aesthetic form, in which he envisioned a transmodern world to come in terms of *cosmopolitan being* and *border thinking*.

Decoloniality of Power, Knowledge, and Being

To unpack the decoloniality of power, knowledge, and being, I will begin with a survey of the historical reason that drives world modernity as liberation praxis, according to Quijano. After that, I shall discuss (a) *pluriversal politics as a decoloniality of power*, (b) *ecologies of knowledges as a decoloniality of knowledge*, and (c) *decolonial aesthesis as a decoloniality of being*.

Quijano (1989) defines *historical reason* as follows:

In the countries of the south, the predominant idea of rationality was formed, especially in the debate concerning society, primarily in relation to the definition of ends. These ends were those of the liberation of society from all inequality, injustice, despotism, and obscurantism. In other words, these ends were defined against the existing arrangements of power. There, modernity was conceived as a promise of rational social existence as well as a promise of freedom, of equity, of solidarity, of the continuous improvement of the material conditions of *these* forms of social existence, not of any other. This is what came to be recognized from that time forward as "historical reason." (p. 153, emphasis in original)

Quijano is critical of not only modernization's instrumental reason but also "the prophets of postmodernity and of antimodernity" who "celebrate the funeral of the liberationist promises of historical reason and its specific form of modernity" (p. 155). This liberationist modernity of which Quijano speaks is the one sublated in Dussel's term: transmodernity. On the other hand, for Quijano, modernization—that is, modernity/coloniality—is premised on domination through "the logic of technology and the discourse of power" (p. 155), manifestations of instrumental (read: bourgeois) reason.

As a concept, the genealogy of historical reason may be traced back to Georg Wilhelm Friedrich Hegel's (1837/1975) *Lectures on the Philosophy of World History*. Still, Quijano probably encountered the notion through the work of José Ortega y Gasset, who influenced many Latin American theorists. Ortega y Gasset, for his part, most likely encountered the idea through the writing of Wilhelm Dilthey. For an overview of the concept of historical reason in contemporary French philosophy, the reader is encouraged to review Andrew Gibson's (2012) *Intermittency*, which explores the radical thinking of Alain Badiou and Jacques Rancière, among others.

Hegel wrote, "*The only thought which philosophy brings with it is the simple idea of reason—the idea that reason governs the world, and that world history is therefore a rational process*" (p. 27, emphasis in original). For Hegel, this rational process of divine reason has teleology whose end is the absolute (p. 28). In other words, for him, "*reason rules the world*" (p. 35, emphasis in original), which many have interpreted to mean that history is unilinear and progressive. However, for Hegel, history is a dialectical and cyclical process: "Change is a cyclic process, a repetition of identical phases" (p. 128). According to him, "*World history is the progress of the consciousness of freedom*" (p. 54, emphasis in original). Consequently, the rational progress of modernity is not the technological progress of modernization.

Herbert Marcuse (1955) takes up this theme from Hegel in *Reason and Revolution* when he writes:

> How does Hegel resolve the apparent contradiction [between universality and particularity]? There can be no question that the needs and interests of individuals are the levers of all historical action, and that in history it is the individual's fulfillment that should come to pass. Something else asserts itself, however—*historical reason*. As they follow out their own interests, individuals promote the progress of mind, that is, perform a universal task that advances freedom. Hegel cites the example of Caesar's struggle for power. In his overthrow of the traditional form of Roman state, Caesar was certainly driven by ambition; but, in satisfying his personal drives he fulfilled "a necessary destiny in the history of Rome and of the world"; through his actions, he achieved a higher, more rational form of political organization. (pp. 229–30, emphasis added)

Before turning to the thinking of Ortega y Gasset, I must briefly address Wilhelm Dilthey's critique of historical reason (cf. Ermarth, 1978), which was his response to Immanuel Kant's *Critique of Pure Reason*. For Dilthey, a critique of historical reason is "the attempt 'to examine the nature and condition of historical consciousness'" (as cited in Marcotte-Chenard, 2022, p. 4). According to Sophie Marcotte-Chenard (2022), "The Diltheyian critique of history should be understood as the equivalent, for metaphysics of history, of the Kantian critique against the systems of dogmatic metaphysics" (p. 4).

Furthermore, Marcotte-Chenard identifies the three elements of Dilthey's project: "a) the attention to the particular, b) the insistence on the situated character of the knowing subject and on lived experience, and c) the primacy of historical consciousness" (p. 5). Dilthey's critique is arguably in alignment with Quijano's conception of historical reason, for it "involves a critique of ahistorical and deductive modes of apprehending socio-historical reality, which subsume particular instances under general categories and make us miss the richness of historical reality" (p. 9).

In *History as a System*, Ortega y Gasset (1962) writes:

> The expression "historical reason" must be understood in all the rigor of the term: not an extrahistorical reason which appears to be fulfilled in history

but, literally, *a substantive reason constituted by what has happened to man* [*sic*] ... Until now what we have had of reason has not been historical and what we have had of history has not been rational. Historical reason is, then, *ratio*, *logos*, a rigorous concept ... In opposing it to physico-mathematical reason there is no question of granting a license to irrationalism. On the contrary, historical reason is still more rational than physical reason, more rigorous, more exigent ... Historical reason, on the contrary, accepts nothing as a mere fact: it makes every fact fluid in the *fieri* whence it comes, it *sees* how the fact takes place. (pp. 231–2, emphasis in original)

Ortega y Gasset's argument is grounded in a humanistic sensibility regarding the pluriversality of subjective reason in history. His claim resonates with Touraine's critique of modernity (i.e., its exclusion of subjectivity). I also think that historical reason is echoed in Said's (1983) essay on secular criticism, particularly with his notion of worldliness: "Texts are worldly, to some degree they are events, and, even when they appear to deny it, they are nevertheless a part of the social world, human life, and of course the historical moments in which they are located and interpreted" (p. 4).

But, for Said, not only texts but also intellectuals are worldly, and "by virtue of that worldliness itself, the intellectual's social identity should involve something more than strengthening those aspects of the culture that require mere affirmation and orthodox compliancy from its members" (p. 24). Said describes the dialectical and liberationist logic of historical reason in that quote, and later, he emphasizes the materiality of worldliness. In other words, while our worldliness as human subjects is materially bound to a specific time and place, we also have an ethical responsibility to use our historical reason critically toward a liberationist end.

In *Historical Reason*, Ortega y Gasset (1984) writes:

Pure reason (which, as we noticed, ended its attempt to deduce everything according to pure logic by basing itself on the narrative of an event: the collision of atoms) must be replaced by narrative reason. *Today* man [sic] is as he is because *yesterday* he was something else. Therefore, to understand what he is today we have only to relate what he was *yesterday*. That is enough, and here we have, come to light, just what we are doing here. This narrative reason is "historical reason." (p. 118, emphasis in original)

Ortega y Gasset's equation of historical reason with narrative reason is edifying, for it reaffirms the narrative dimension of human subjectivity (*homo narrans*), the dimension of speech and writing, which is central for both Ibn Rushd and Chahine in the form of poetic reason. In other words, the project of historical reason—as a project of using reason as a means toward liberatory ends—is, to some extent, a narrativizing project. Decoloniality involves telling a different story about the past in the present to prefigure a more liberatory future. In the next three sections, I shall retell decolonial narratives about power, knowledge, and being. As far as Chahine is concerned, the question is why he chose to tell the story of Ibn Rushd in 1997. In other words, what was his historical reason?

Pluriversal Politics

In pluriversal politics, power arises from not only democratic legitimacy but also radical relationality; this is the inverse of modern/colonial politics with its authoritarian techniques of administration through oppression and violence. In decolonial theory, pluriversality has been put forth as an alternative to universality, a deceptive concept that assumes the false universality of Euromodern provinciality. According to this false universality, non-European cinema is "world cinema" instead of simply cinema because its cinematic worldliness—more specifically, its transmodern aesthetic representation of the link between the singular and the pluriversal—is negated by the modern system and rendered Other.

Euro-American subjects do not consider non-European cinema to be as universal as their cinematic productions. Therefore, given the Global North's lack of recognition of the cinematic worldliness of filmic masterpieces from the Global South, the concept of pluriversality must replace the false universality of (Euro-American) cinema, which echoes Mignolo's (2007) point about "*pluriversality as a universal project*" (pp. 452–3, emphasis in original). I will argue in the next section that the *radical humanism* of Chahine's transmodern cinema is a form of pluriversality as a universal project.

The universal project of pluriversality is a bottom-up version of the Non-Aligned Movement; it is an internationalist solidarity campaign among the damned of the world: "What each diverse local history has in common with others is the fact that they all have to deal with the unavoidable presence of the modern/colonial world and its power differentials, which start with racial classification and end up ranking the planet" (Mignolo, 2007, p. 497).

According to Arturo Escobar (2020), the pluriverse "is a world where many worlds fit" (p. ix). In his book, Escobar distinguishes between modernist politics and pluriversal politics, as well as the relationship between the two:

> Multiple ways exist for those of us who operate on the basis of modernist politics to contribute to pluriversal politics even if not embracing ontological politics explicitly—for instance, modernist struggles for economic democratization, for depatriarchalization and the end of racism and homophobia, for environmental justice, and academic critiques. A substantial amount of resistance to injustices and inequities fits the bill. That said, it is also important to recognize that many modernist forms of politics are counterproductive in relation to pluriversal politics; they reproduce and strengthen, rather than undermine, the modernist ontology of separation from which they stem. This is especially the case with liberal forms. (p. xv)

Pluriversal politics is "an ontological politics toward the pluriverse" (p. x) or a politics of "radical interdependence" (p. xvi), which aims "to create conditions favorable to the flourishing of the pluriverse, other ways of world making. Many groups currently rebelling against developmentalist extractivism are resisting this One-World World; they are instances of the pluriverse rising up" (p. 27). *Radical relationality* is at the heart of pluriversal politics, and it signifies "the fact that all entities that make up the world are so deeply interrelated that they have no intrinsic, separate existence by themselves" (p. xiii). Modernist politics, on the other hand, is premised on "the ontology of separation" (p. xiv). Was al-Andalus an instantiation of pluriversal politics? Perhaps this is one of the questions that Chahine's *al-Maṣīr* raises. Can the Arab national project be resignified, in pluriversal terms, as Arab internationalism?

Climate breakdown, for instance, existed neither in the pluriversal worlds of Indigenous tribes on Turtle Island nor in the Caliphate of Córdoba; climate breakdown is a function of the false dichotomy of "man" versus nature, wherein "man" designates a Christian, male, bourgeois, and Euromodern master who gets to dominate everything in the world subsumed under the category of "nature." In the context of colonialism, the category of "nature" included "land belonging to no one" and attached to near-infinite resources, animals, plants, minerals, and sub-/non-human "savages"; in other words, things to be extracted or exploited for the sake of primitive accumulation—the primary condition for racial capitalist modernization.

Ecologies of Knowledges

Boaventura de Sousa Santos (2014) writes about "epistemologies of the South," which he defines as "a set of inquiries into the construction and validation of knowledge born in struggle, of ways of knowing developed by social groups as part of their resistance against the systematic injustices and oppressions caused by capitalism, colonialism, and patriarchy" (p. x). For de Sousa Santos, "*subaltern cosmopolitan reason*" is "the reason that grounds the epistemologies of the South" (p. 164, emphasis in original). Subaltern cosmopolitan reason (cf. historical reason) involves what de Sousa Santos calls "postabyssal thinking," which "starts from the recognition that social exclusion in its broadest sense takes very different forms according to whether it is determined by an abyssal or a nonabyssal line" (p. 133).

The *abyssal line* is the line "dividing metropolitan from colonial societies decades after the end of historical colonialism. Such a line divides social reality in such a profound way that whatever lies on the other side of the line remains invisible or utterly irrelevant" (pp. 70–1). The abyssal line is more than a geopolitical line separating the Global North from the Global South; it is also an ontological line demarcating who is in the zone of being versus the zone of nonbeing. As such, its epistemological ramifications, often disciplinary, are premised on the colonial binary logic of civilizational knowledge (science) versus savage ways of knowing (religion). As such, whereas Descartes is typically framed as a modern philosopher, Ibn Rushd is often positioned as a religious thinker. De Sousa Santos adds:

> The recognition of the persistence of abyssal thinking is thus the *conditio sine qua non* to start thinking and acting beyond it. Without such recognition, critical thinking will remain a derivative thinking that will go

on reproducing the abyssal lines, no matter how antiabyssal it proclaims itself. Postabyssal thinking, on the contrary, is a nonderivative thinking [cf. border thinking]; it involves a radical break with modern Western ways of thinking and acting. In our time, to think in nonderivative terms means to think from the perspective of the other side of the line, precisely because the other side of the line has been the realm of the unthinkable in Western modernity. (p. 134, emphasis in original)

De Sousa Santos emphasizes the importance of *dual sociology* in hegemonic knowledge production: "A sociology of absences is thus as important as a sociology of presences in the social construction of the destabilizing subjectivity. That dual sociology, which still very much remains to be produced, is at the core of the emancipatory will of the emergent subjectivity" (p. 97). De Sousa Santos underlines the centrality of critical epistemology for subaltern subjectivity to think about the effects of hegemonic epistemology, in particular. For him, the sociology of absences "is the sociology of absent ways of knowing, that is to say, the act of identifying the ways of knowing that hegemonic epistemology reduces to nonexistence" (p. 111).

To counter the sociology of absences, we have the sociology of emergences. The sociology of emergences "consists of replacing the emptiness of the future (according to linear time) with a future of plural and concrete possibilities, utopian and realist at one and the same time and constructed in the present by means of activities of care" (p. 182). The sociology of emergences also entails "radical copresence," which for de Sousa Santos "means that practices and agents on both sides of the abyssal line are contemporaneous granted that there is more than one kind of contemporaneity. Radical copresence means equating simultaneity with contemporaneity, which can only be accomplished if the linear conception of time is abandoned" (p. 191).

In sum, the epistemologies of the South are based on two methods: "ecologies of knowledges and intercultural translation" (p. 188). De Sousa Santos writes, "The ecology of knowledges [e.g., Arab-Islamic philosophy] confronts the logic of the monoculture of scientific knowledge and rigor by identifying other knowledges and criteria of rigor and validity that operate credibly in social practices pronounced nonexistent by metonymic reason" (p. 188). In other words, in the ecology of knowledges, scientific and nonscientific ways of knowing are equally explored; however, de Sousa Santos provides an important caveat:

> The ecology of knowledges does not entail accepting relativism. On the contrary, from the point of view of a pragmatics of social emancipation, relativism, considered as an absence of criteria of hierarchy among knowledges, is an unsustainable position, for it renders impossible any relation between knowledge and the meaning of social transformation. If all the different kinds of knowledge are equally valid as knowledge, every project of social transformation is equally valid or, likewise, equally invalid. The ecology of knowledges aims to create a new kind of relation, a pragmatic relation, between scientific knowledge and other kinds of knowledge. It consists of granting "equality of opportunity" to the different kinds of knowledge involved in ever broader epistemological arguments with a view to maximizing their respective contributions toward building "another possible world," that is to say, a more just and democratic society, as well as one more balanced in its relations with nature. (p. 190)

In addition to the ecology of knowledges, the sociology of emergences also involves *intercultural translation*, which "is the alternative both to the abstract universalism that grounds Western-centric general theories and to the idea of incommensurability between cultures" (p. 212). De Sousa Santos adds:

> Intercultural translation consists of searching for isomorphic concerns and underlying assumptions among cultures, identifying differences and similarities, and developing, whenever appropriate, new hybrid forms of cultural understanding and intercommunication that may be useful in favoring interactions and strengthening alliances among social movements fighting, in different cultural contexts, against capitalism, colonialism, and patriarchy and for social justice, human dignity, or human decency. Intercultural translation questions both the reified dichotomies among alternative knowledges (e.g., indigenous knowledge versus scientific knowledge) and the unequal abstract status of different knowledges (e.g., indigenous knowledge as a valid claim of identity versus scientific knowledge as a valid claim of truth). In sum, the work of translation enables us to cope with diversity and conflict in the absence of a general theory and a commando politics. (pp. 212–13)

Intercultural translation is essential in the project of transmodernity, which is a project of intercultural translation between liberationist modernity and radical exteriority, and as we shall see later, the bridge serves as a metaphor for this method. Moroccan philosopher Abdelkebir Khatibi (2019) explored radical exteriority in his writings through his concept of "other-thought," which he invokes to critique Arab reason:

> That is why here the name "Arab" is, on the one hand, the name of a civilization that is finished in its founding metaphysical element. "Finished" does not mean that this civilization is in reality dead, but that it is incapable of renewing itself as thought, except through the insurgency of an other-thought, which is dialogue with planetary transformations. On the other hand, the name "Arab" designates a war of naming and ideologies, which bring to light the active plurality of the Arab world. (p. 3)

Other-thought is "independent of the political discourse of our time" (p. 5); it is "a gift bestowed by the suffering that seizes its terrible freedom" (p. 6). Khatibi continues:

> What is *necessary* (the duty of an other-thought) is to broaden our freedom to think, to introduce in all dialogue several strategic levers—for example, to eliminate from discourse the absolutes of theology and theocentricism, which shackle the time, space, and edifice of Maghrebi [and other Global Southern] societies. But this is not enough. The dialogue with all thought of difference is monumental. It aims to unsettle all that stupefies us in repetition and reproduction. An other-thought is always a plot, a conspiracy, a perpetual revolt, and a relentless risk. And we are so defenseless in the face of the power of the world. Such is our "history," which will have struck the body. (p. 19, emphasis in original)

Other-thought is equivalent to border thinking, and this link becomes lucid when one considers the location of Morocco on the border with Europe, separated by the Strait of Gibraltar, which is a thirty-six-mile-long channel between Point Cires, Morocco, and Point Marroquí, Spain. It is also worth reflecting on the history of Morocco—and much of al-Maghreb being part of al-Andalus at one point in time. In fact, for a number of intermittent years, Ibn Rushd lived, worked, and eventually died in Marrakesh. al-Andalus challenges our imaginary geography or the abyssal line separating Europe from the non-European world on the basis of cultural difference—the manifest form of colonial difference.

Therefore, other-thought, as a postabyssal praxis, *"works to penetrate the question of nonpower on the one hand and, on the other, to try to go beyond this opposition (power, nonpower) toward a research that would erase itself at the margins of metaphysics"* (p. 25, emphasis in original). Other-thought, a Southern epistemology, is one example of the decoloniality of knowledge, for, as Khatibi writes, "to be decolonized would be the other name of this other-thought, and decolonization would be the silent completion of Western metaphysics. And this is where begins this third speech, this unbinding of Western reason, in its sciences and techniques" (p. 28).

In *al-Maṣīr*, Chahine shines a light on the Other-thought of Ibn Rushd to give voice to a third speech. Egyptian philosopher Mourad Wahba (2006) argues that Ibn Rushd can function as a "bridge" between European and Arab-Islamic philosophies, mainly because of his paradoxical status. Elsewhere, he writes, "Islamic civilization crystallized in [Averroism], whereas Averroes has been totally alienated from Islamic culture" (Wahba, 1980, p. 260). This is why Chahine returns to Ibn Rushd and highlights his Islamic humanism, particularly for an Egyptian audience in the 1990s. Chahine is prefiguring a transmodern utopia, wherein the historical reason of Averroism (*Rushdiya*) is driving the Arab internationalist project to come.

In a sense, *al-Maṣīr* is Chahine's answer to Wahba's question: "To what extent can the present-day Islamic world benefit from [Ibn Rushd's] philosophy in the realization of historical changes as had been the case in the development of human civilization in the European Christian world?" (p. 260). Both Wahba and Chahine believe that Ibn Rushd's philosophy has a "creative role" to play today "in enriching and enhancing human civilization," especially in the Arab world. I hope the reader will choose to agree with this premise. The alternative is retreating into either totality or exteriority while conceding defeat in the realm of intercultural translation. Even if dialogue is impossible, this transmodern intervention is necessary as a liberatory path beyond the apparatus of racial capitalism and its oppressive/violent techniques.

Aesthetics of Liberation

Decolonial Poiēsis/Aísthēsis

According to Clive Cazeaux (2000), the understanding of "aesthetics as the study of beauty and, in particular, the beautiful in art ... originates in the eighteenth century with the appearance of the 'modern (Cartesian) individual'" (p. xv). Two German thinkers are often credited for making aesthetics a major branch of philosophy: Alexander Baumgarten and Immanuel Kant (p. 3). Instead of surveying the history of aesthetic theories, I shall hone in on a couple of debates regarding the relationship between aesthetics and politics.

In terms of the "distribution of the sensible" or "the system of self-evident facts of sense perception" (p. 7), Jacques Rancière (2004) identifies three major artistic regimes: (1) "an ethical regime of the image," (2) the "poetic—or representative—regime of the arts," and (3) the "aesthetic regime of the arts" (pp. 16–18). Rancière associates the first two regimes with Plato and Aristotle, respectively, and argues that the "aesthetic regime of the arts [which is around two hundred years old] is the regime that strictly identifies art in the singular and frees it from any specific rule, from any hierarchy of the arts, subject matter, and genres" (pp. 18–19).

Consequently, Rancière asserts that the aesthetic regime of the arts "is the true name for what is designated by the incoherent label 'modernity'" (p. 19). For Rancière, modernism "seems to have been deliberately invented to prevent a clear understanding of the transformations of art and its relationships with other spheres of collective experience" (p. 21). For example, while modernism supposedly indicates a historical shift from figurative to nonfigurative representation in painting, realism is a modernist movement that "does not in any way mean the valorization of resemblance but rather the destruction of the structures within which it functioned" (p. 19). The question of historicizing aesthetic modernity is further complicated by the fact that Islamic art, for instance, was nonfigurative centuries before European artists leaped outside of *mīmēsis* (Shabout, 2007).

"The idea of modernity," Rancière continues, "would like there to be only one meaning and direction in history, whereas the temporality specific to the aesthetic regime of the arts is *co-presence of heterogenous temporalities*" (p. 21, emphasis added). Along similar lines, Adonis (1990) shows that the modernity of Arab poetics complicates the linear historicity presupposed by most European theorists; as I will show later, Arab modernity—and perhaps modernity as such—is nonlinear or anachronic. When considering the relationship between aesthetics and politics, Rancière writes:

> The history of the relations between *political parties* and *aesthetic movements* is first of all the history of a confusion ... between these two ideas of the *avant-garde*, which are in fact two different ideas of *political subjectivity*: *the archi-political idea of a party*, that is to say the idea of a form of political intelligence that sums up the essential conditions for change, and *the meta-political idea of global political subjectivity*, the idea of the potentiality inherent in the innovative sensible modes of experience that anticipate a community to come. (p. 25, emphasis added)

As an aesthetic conception, the meta-political dimension is the political dimension worth exploring vis-à-vis Chahine's transmodern aesthetics. Chahine was aware of the limitation of archi-politics when it comes to aesthetics:

> I think that politics are inevitable. Politics control our lives the way world economics influences our local economy and how that influences our social life. We are managed by everything that is happening in the world—it's globalization ... But the point is, in film, you can't bring politics out as a slogan. You have a drama first, a drama of people being influenced by a certain type of political situation, but the drama comes first. (as cited in Massad, 1999, p. 88)

The meta-politics of transmodern aesthetics allow us to bypass what Frederic Jameson calls "the Realism/Modernism controversy" (p. 219), which was a debate among theorists and practitioners associated with the Frankfurt School, such as Theodor Adorno, Walter Benjamin, Ernest Bloch, Bertolt Brecht, and Georg Lukás (2010). In sum, their discussion revolved around the relationship between aesthetic forms and radical politics; in other words, they wanted to determine whether realism or modernism was more revolutionary regarding their respective politico-aesthetic effects on proletarian spectators/

listeners. Rancière, however, explodes this debate by arguing that realism is a form of modernism. In the context of Egyptian cinema, realism is one of the dominant aesthetic forms.

For Rancière, "equality is actually the condition required for being able to think politics" (p. 48), and it "only generates politics when it is implemented in the specific form of a particular case of dissensus" (p. 49). "Politics," therefore, "exists when the figure of a specific subject is constituted, a supernumerary subject in relation to the calculated number of groups, places, and functions in a society. This is summed up in the concept of the *dêmos*" (pp. 47–8, emphasis in original).

For the remainder of this section, I will argue that Chahine's cinematic aesthetics—an instantiation of modern Arab art (cf. Shabout, 2007)—can be characterized as transmodern, for his cinema embodies two types of modernity: *the totality of European aesthetics* and *the exteriority of Arab poetics*. I will also consider the liberatory (or meta-political) dimension of Chahine's transmodern poetics/aesthetics, particularly concerning relevant theorizations of decolonial poiēsis/aísthēsis.

Following Rancière (p. 80), some critical questions include: what kind of common world is *al-Maṣīr* producing or of which it is a product? What are the film's forms of perception, description, and interpretation of this common world? These critical questions pertain to Chahine's radical *vision*, which, as far as modern Arab art is concerned, is more important than formal *technique*. Khatibi argues, "Techniques and methods are available and easy to import, but they are not the goal of the work of art. The goal is for the artist to have a unique vision" (as cited in Shabout, 2007, p. 44). In transmodern aesthetics, aesthetic techniques are adopted alongside radical visionary poetics.

The concepts of poiēsis and aísthēsis can be traced back to ancient Greek philosophy, wherein poiēsis signifies formation (i.e., making, creating, or producing something); it eventually became *ars* (i.e., art) in Latin, as in "skill" (Mignolo, as cited in Gaztambide-Fernández, 2014, p. 200). According to Mignolo, "Poiesis needs a particular executioner, the poet that is able to, instead of making a shoe or building a house, 'make' a narrative that captures the senses and emotions of a lot of people" (p. 203).

Aísthēsis, on the other hand, "refers to lived felt experience, knowledge as it is obtained through the senses" (Cazeaux, 2000, p. xv); that is, aísthēsis is an embodied sensibility, which may be described as affective as opposed to cognitive. Decolonial theorists (e.g., Mignolo & Vázquez, 2013; Ramos, 2018; Vallega, 2014a; Vázquez, 2020) have reclaimed the notion of aísthēsis in particular, but from the exterior perspective of non-European alterity, to explore "pre-rational" modern sensibilities (Vallega, 2014a), which inform not only aesthetics and politics but also ethics and poetics, that is, the arts *qua* "ways of doing and making" (Rancière, 2004, p. 16).

Miguel Rojas-Sotelo (2014) has documented the history of "decolonial aesthetics." While Adolfo Albán Achinte coined the phrase in 2003, decolonial aesthetics as a movement commenced with a 2010 exhibit in Bogotá, Colombia, on the topic, followed by another one the next year at Duke University. In 2011, the Transnational Decolonial Institute published the Decolonial Aesthetics Manifesto on its website. In 2013, Walter Mignolo and Rolando Vázquez coedited a dossier on decolonial aísthēsis, published by Social Text. The dossier included the Manifesto, among other essays by different intellectuals, curators, and artists. At stake for Mignolo and Vázquez (2013) in the dossier is what they call the geopolitics of knowing, sensing, and believing. They add:

> By opting for the geopolitics of knowing, sensing and believing we are not aiming at essentialisms but at pluri-versalism: each local history is universal. The belief that uni-versal is one is the fiction of Western Civilization and modern aestheTics. Modern aestheTics had its point of origination in Europe, it is regional, local but assumes the right to be ONE universal AMONG other regional and local universals. Pluriversality is composed of many universalities and it departs from decolonizing the Eurocentered fiction of one universality—that of its own local and regional history. What we present here is the work in progress of the decolonial option, or options in plural if you wish, but decolonial at the end.

In his seminal essay on delinking, Mignolo (2007) argues for the necessity of a decolonial shift, on the level of epistemology, from a theo-/ego-politics of knowledge to a geo-/body-politics of knowledge. He writes:

> I take Theo-logy as the historical and dominant frame of knowledge in the modern/colonial world from the sixteenth to the first half of the eighteenth century … When Western politics of knowledge began to be imposed

in Asia and Africa, in the nineteenth century, Europe has already gone through an internal transformation. The sovereignty of the subject began to be felt at the beginning of the seventeenth century (Cervantes, Bacon, Shakespeare, Descartes) and the questioning of Theology open up the doors for a displacement, within Europe, from the Theo-logical to the Ego-logical politics of knowledge and understanding. (pp. 459–60)

In contrast, "the geo-politics of knowledge names the historical location ... and authority of loci of enunciations that had been negated by the dominance and hegemony of both the theo-logical and ego-logical politics of knowledge and understanding" (p. 460). Furthermore, "the body-politics of knowledge includes the re-inscription, per Fanon for example, of the history inscribed in the black body in a cosmology dominated by the white body underneath the theo- and ego-politics of knowledge" (p. 484). The geo-/body-politics of knowledge presupposes "an *identity based on politics* (and not a *politics based on identity*)" (p. 492, emphasis in original).

The rational ego cogito/conquiro—that is, the modern subject of the theo-/ego-politics of knowledge—exhibits an unconscious affinity to *colonial aísthēsis*, which actualizes itself in terms of modernization's instrumental reason. At the heart of instrumental reason is a sensibility for domination over nature, that is, everything/everyone considered to be "savage," such as the premodern "primitives" living before the temporality of, and the nonmodern "barbarians" living exterior to the spatiality of, Euromodern "civilization." This is the same instrumental reason of (colonial) film theory, which negates non-European cinema and decolonial film theory.

On the other hand, the transmodern subject of the geo-/ego-politics of knowledge exhibits an unconscious affinity to a *decolonial aísthēsis*; he or she is driven by world historical reason toward collective liberation. A transmodern/decolonial sensibility eschews ideological ethnocentrism in favor of material worldliness: "one civilization, many cultures" (Wahba & Abousenna, 2010). This material worldliness is pluriversal: "a world where many worlds fit" (Escobar, 2020, p. ix). To put it differently, the transmodern subject of decolonial aísthēsis (e.g., Chahine) envisions, through its singularity of being, a pluriversal world (e.g., al-Andalus) where many ethico-politico-aesthetic worlds fit. The singularity of Chahine's cosmopolitan being is a function of his border thinking.

Transmodern Aesthetics of Liberation

Alejandro Vallega (2014b) has written about "an aesthetics of liberation out of Latin American experience." I wish to stretch his theorizing to consider transmodern aesthetics of liberation in general and aesthetics of liberation out of the Arab experience in particular. Vallega begins with an epigraph from Quijano: "It is in the aesthetic where the transfigurations of possible historical totalities are prefigured" (p. 125). This quote sets the terrain for aesthetics as a site of critique and resistance vis-à-vis the Eurocentric coloniality of power/ knowledge. Vallega writes:

> My focus in this essay is on the recognition of a liberatory aesthetic level of experience found in Latin American consciousness. On the one hand, in light of this aesthetic level of experience in its distinctness one may begin to undo the tradition of domination and dependence that obscures the positive overlapping of Western traditions and traditions distinct from it. At the same time, this engagement with the aesthetic dimension of experience also makes possible the opening of a space for the affirmation and recognition of other ways of thinking and ways of being that to date have, for the most part been excluded, ignored, and wasted. (p. 126)

Following Dussel and Quijano, Vallega argues that the coloniality of power/ knowledge is premised on a colonial aesthetic sensibility regarding temporality, or the "coloniality of time." The coloniality of time presupposes a "single historical timeline" (p. 8). He adds, "Whatever is meaningful depends on its place within the single timeline. This means that the very recognition of forms of knowledge … remains under the requirement of the movement or progress of the single timeline" (p. 136). The idea of the "primitive" is a function of the coloniality of time, for the "primitive" is framed as existing before history or time; hence, modernization is introduced as the civilizing mechanism through which the "primitive" can be caught up with the progressive timeline of Euromodernity. From a decolonial— and, I must add, Marxist—perspective, history (as the history of class struggles) is dialectically related to collective liberation. There is nothing historical about oppression and violence; they are part of prehistory. The linear model of historical progress then is nothing but a modern myth, which ideologically sutures the ongoing material realities of oppression: class struggle, racism, and sexism.

The decoloniality of time, on the other hand, involves multiple historical timelines and a nonlinear aesthetic sensibility regarding temporality. Vallega writes, "This sense of overlapping temporalities introduces an ana-chronic sense of time and history in that the simultaneous asymmetry of temporalities situates them (temporality and history) beyond a single line of development or ordering of lives and sense of existence" (pp. 8–9). This ana-chronic sensibility is present in the temporality of Arab poetics and the history of Arab modernity, which is akin to a parallel universe vis-à-vis the timeline of Euromodernity—a function of the exteriority of the Arab-Islamic world. For instance, the Islamic Golden Age (622–1258) overlapped with the European Dark Ages (476–1000); also, while the European Renaissance began around 1300, the Arab Renaissance (*al-nahḍa*) started in the late nineteenth century—for a critique of *al-nahḍa* historiography, cf. Wagner (2022).

Furthermore, Adonis (1990) traces Arab modernity to the eighth century, which speaks to the ana-chronic dimension of poetic sensibility beyond current historical debates regarding "tradition" versus "modernity." The poetical order is dialectically both traditional and modern. For Adonis, the modernity of Arab poetics means two things: "first, renewal, which was not a rejection of the pre-Islamic tradition, but an affirmation of renewed life; and, second, artistic and intellectual methods of organization in the aesthetic context of this renewal, at the levels of both vision and expression" (p. 98). In other words, modernity for Adonis is both nonlinear and not exclusively European; additionally, it is atemporal although still historical:

> Modernity was both of time and outside time: of time because it is rooted in the movement of history, in the creativity of humanity … and outside time because it is a vision which includes in it all times and cannot only be recorded as a chronological event. (p. 99)

Like Quijano, Adonis distinguishes between modernity, which he associates with artistic creativity, and modernization, which has to do with scientific or technological progress. For Adonis, contemporary Arab poets live in a state of "double siege" (p. 81), between a rock (Arab-Islamic tradition) and a hard place (Euromodernity). This state of "double dependency" (p. 80) results in an identity crisis for most Arabs in general, which, for Adonis, is based on an alienating false choice, to begin with.

In other words, Adonis sheds light on a third way, which Ibn Rushd exemplified. In terms of tradition, "What we should take hold of and imitate is the flame of questioning which animated our ancestors, so that we can complement their work with a new vision and new approaches to knowledge" (p. 90). In terms of Euromodernity, he distinguishes between learning "from the creative energy of the West and its intellectual inventions [to] construct a dialogue with them" (p. 91) and rejecting the politics and ideology of Western imperialism.

Since I addressed the decoloniality of time through *anachronic temporality* and *historical reason*, I wish now to turn to the decoloniality of space through the concepts of *borderland spatiality* and *radical exteriority*. In the preface to *Borderlands/La Frontera*, Anzaldúa (1987) writes, "Borderlands are physically present wherever two or more cultures edge each other, where people of different races occupy the same territory, where under, lower, middle and upper classes touch, where the space between two individuals shrinks with intimacy." Anzaldúa was thinking about the Texas–US Southwest/Mexican border specifically, but I wish to extend her analysis to al-Andalus as a borderland space that disrupts the clear geopolitical distinction between Europe and its Other (the non-European world). Anzaldúa writes that "border culture" is a "third country" formed from "the lifeblood of two worlds merging" (p. 3).

In a similar vein, Homi Bhabha (1990) explores the "third space" of hybridity, which "displaces the histories that constitute it, and sets up new structures of authority, new political initiatives, which are inadequately understood through received wisdom" (p. 211). Going back to al-Andalus, Mohamad Ballan (2019) asserts:

> Covering a period of over 250 years, this polity [the Nasrid Kingdom of Granda] straddled the borderland between Islam and Latin Christendom. By the early 8th/14th century … the kingdom encompassed one of the most populous, urban and diverse populations in late medieval Spain, being home to a large community of Andalusi Muslims, a significant garrison of North African troops, a considerable Jewish population, as well as various communities of Spanish and Italian Christians. (p. 23)

Ballan cites Andalusian polymath Ibn al-Khaṭīb, who conceived of the city of Granada to be "chosen by God as a borderland (*thaghr*) of Islam" (p. 309, emphasis in original). al-Andalus was a borderland because it was "the one spot on earth containing all other places within it" (Anzaldúa, 2015, p. 57). While Muslims no longer rule al-Andalus today, the cultural influence of Islam can still be detected not only through magnificent architectural feats (e.g., Alhambra palace) but also through the many Spanish toponyms for villages, rivers, or mountains of Arabic origin.

The decoloniality of space then corresponds to a decolonial aesthetic sensibility regarding spatiality and comes into focus through Anzaldúa's (2015) praxis of "border arte," which aims at healing colonialism's wounds. For example, being Arab designates more than an ethnicity; an Arab is often an Arabic-speaking hybrid subject who may or may not be also Muslim. This link between Arab subjectivity and the Arabic language is crucial, particularly when thinking about or practicing modern Arab poetics/aesthetics.

Modern Arab art is border art, in a sense, for it is a secular rupture from Islamic art, which negotiates its artistic identity concerning European aesthetics and Arab poetics (Shabout, 2007). Following Anzaldúa, we can conceive of modern Arab cinema as "the locus of resistance, of rupture, of implosion and explosion, and of putting together the fragments and creating a new assemblage" (p. 49). Modern Arab cinema is a spatial distortion within Euclidean geometry and the Cartesian coordinate system; modern Arab cinema is border cinema, a counter-cartography. Arab artists, mostly border people in North Africa and West Asia, "live in a state of nepantla. The Nahuatl word for an in-between state" (p. 56).

Arabs are usually not considered African or Asian, even though they mostly live in Africa and Asia. Many of them live near the Mediterranean, which links them to Europe. The in-between, or third, space of Arabness affords the possibility of actualizing a transmodern subjectivity grounded in a rich poetic tradition, but this potential was historically thwarted—at least, partially—by the failed project of Arab nationalism and continues to be frustrated by the afterlives of that political failure (e.g., civil wars and failed states). Islamic fundamentalism has typically inserted itself in the political vacuums afforded by instabilities in the Arab world since decolonization. Its secular alternative typically takes the form of military dictatorship. In effect, militarism and fundamentalism are two sides of the same authoritarian coin.

Following Vallega (2014a), the question of Arab identity is not only a question of the Arabs' identifications with the Islamic tradition or the Arabic language but also a question of their radical exteriority to themselves and to one another, which opens up the space for a pluriversal politics of difference based on *singularity-in-comradeship*. Thinking in radical exteriority, for Vallega, is a function of "the aesthetic dimension of being in radical exteriority" (p. 9), which entails a "pre-linguistic experience of proximity" (p. 11) vis-à-vis the Other of the Other. Thinking in radical exteriority (i.e., border thinking) then means

> thinking *from* and *with* the living configurations and excluded lineages and histories of those considered peripheral and ultimately meaningless by Western calculative and instrumental rationalism and its production of knowledge and power under the ideals of capitalism, colonialism, neoliberalism, and globalism. (p. 6, emphasis in original)

Vallega adds, "The appearing of the other marks a movement—a moment when exterior peripheral life rises forth in its potential creativity, in a moment that is not individual but of a people, of a community, in its creative force" (p. 64). In other words, the social identifications that amount to solidarity around Arab internationalism would not be possible without the creative sensibilities arising from radical exteriority, which allow for the quantum leap from the singular to the pluriversal, or from ethics to politics via aesthetics, which I have come to call *singularity-in-comradeship*.

Consequently, the radical exteriority of Arab poetics functions as a social tie and indicates an aesthetic sensibility grounded in anachronic temporality and borderland spatiality, for Arab modernity is nonlinear and Islamic humanism has no borders. In sum, *the Arabic unconscious is structured like a poem*. My phrase (the Arabic unconscious) points to the nature of the unconscious, which is structured like a language, as Lacan shows. I am not, however, speaking of a homogenous, or essentialist, Arab collective unconscious shared by ethnic Arabs in the Orientalist tradition of Raphael Patai's (1973) *The Arab Mind*.

Conversely, the Arabic unconscious is the heterogeneous and existentialist unconscious of any Arabic speaker; the Arabic unconscious is the poetic discourse of Arab modernity—a discourse exterior to the totality of European aesthetics and negated by it; therefore, the Arabic unconscious is the discourse of the Other of the Other.

Decolonial Film Theory

Theory is a lens through which we can foreground some aspects of a phenomenon while blurring others. Theory is also a filter that colors, distorts, and stylizes how we perceive anything. A film is a complex artifact—a mass-produced/consumed audio-visual commodity—comprised of five formal elements (narrative, mise-en-scène, cinematography, sound, and editing); therefore, film theory is a tool used by the critic—or the spectator—to highlight the significance of these formal elements of film from a particular theoretical standpoint (cf. Andrew, 1976; Lapsley & Westlake, 1988; Stam, 2000).

In my view, there a two central tasks in decolonial film theory: (1) choosing to critique radical films produced in the Global South or produced by racialized subjects in the Global North and (2) critiquing these radical films through the lens of decoloniality. As such, the decolonial film theorist is interested in the worlding of film theory by emphasizing the cinematic worldliness of non-European cinema—its transmodernity. My decision to critique an Egyptian film (*al-Maṣīr*), which bears an Arabic title, is meant to decenter Euro-American, particularly Hollywood, cinema and to marginalize the hegemony of (colonial) film theory.

As far as I am concerned, the true center of the cinematic universe is cinephilia, or the love of cinema. I cannot think of a bigger cinephile than Chahine, who loved cinema because he loved life, beauty, music, theater, dance, love, and so on. Any cinephile should hypothetically be interested in enjoyable filmic masterpieces regardless of *where* they were produced or *who* produced them. However, this ideal is challenged by certain concrete facts: a profit-driven film industry within the context of racial capitalism. The film industry's material reality—its class struggle, for example—is typically covered over ideologically by aesthetic formulas that provide fantasmatic answers to unresolved political questions. In the words of Frederic Jameson, the kernel of this ideological cinema—particularly as crystallized in the popular genre of disaster films—is that "it is easier to imagine the end of the world than the end of capitalism."

The racial capitalist ideology sutures its central deadlock (class struggle) and projects this impossible contradiction in terms of cultural clashes between totality and exteriority. Cultural difference is the manifest form of colonial difference, and it explains why non-European cinema is designated "world cinema" or why non-European philosophy is considered "thought." My effort here has been to show that Chahine contributed to cinema just as much as Ibn Rushd contributed to philosophy, even if it was from the perspective of exteriority.

Decolonial film theory rejects the oppressive designations and classifications of (colonial) film theory vis-à-vis non-European cinema, for they follow the oppressive logic of instrumental reason. The legacy of instrumental reason includes the oppression and violence of modern colonialism/imperialism since the fifteenth century: numerous genocides and ethnocides, the transatlantic slave trade, and environmental breakdown, to name a few. Furthermore, the category of "world cinema" implies "savagery" or a cultural lag behind "civilized" cinema; the label is a function of the Eurocentric logics of spatial and temporal colonial difference, wherein the "barbarian" Other is framed as outside "civilization" (Euromodernity) and the "primitive" Other is positioned as developmentally stuck in premodernity—before the beginning of History.

However, historical reason, a feature of modernity *sans* coloniality, signifies that reason and liberation go hand in hand. Reason was central for Ibn Rushd and Youssef Chahine; I also find it essential. Paget Henry (2000) calls this Other reason, which was covered over by Euromodernity, "Caliban's reason." If we—cinephiles—are interested in the liberatory potential of transmodern cinema, we must begin from this Other reason, which is exterior to Euromodernity and yet in dialogue with it. That is where I begin in the next chapter: the life and philosophy of Ibn Rushd (1126–1198), the subject of Youssef Chahine's (1997) *al-Maṣīr*.

Decolonial film theory follows the three steps of decolonial methodology:

1) To show [the] genealogy [of hegemonic concepts] in western modernity that allows us to transform the universal validity claims of western concepts and turn them into concepts historically situated; 2) To show their coloniality, that is how they have functioned to erase, silence, denigrate other ways of understanding and relating to the world; and finally 3) To build on this grounds the decolonial option, as a non-normative space, as a space open to the plurality of alternatives. (Mignolo & Vázquez, 2013, pp. 7–8)

I will share more about the "savage" methodology of decolonial film theory in Part 2. During World Cinema Fund Day in 2021, Viola Shafik shared her thoughts on decolonizing cinema. She argued that cinema appeared during European colonialism and was part of the nation formation project. For her, cinema is intrinsically linked to Othering and the Gaze. She argues that coloniality has been there since the beginning of cinema. For example, the Lumière Brothers sent filmmakers to the Orient to film Oriental subjects for the Gaze of a European audience. This Gaze framed the colonized Other as exotic to affirm European civilization's supposed superiority and justify its civilizing mission in the non-European world.

Shafik (2021) addresses Third Cinema in the context of the decolonization of Africa and Asia and the Non-Aligned Movement. She then talks about the importance of guerilla filmmaking and film collectives in Global Southern liberationist movements. Shafik suggests decolonizing cinema through Indigenous filmmaking and grassroots collectives that employ a different language, structure, and perspective. Finally, she cautions against decolonial cinema being co-opted, or recolonized, by the neoliberal film market and rebranded as "auteur cinema," which is how Chahine's cinema is typically theorized by Euro-American film theorists. However, in Part 2, I will attempt to complexify our theorization of Chahine's transmodern cinema after introducing the humanistic philosophy of Ibn Rushd.

Part 2

Decoloniality and *al-Maṣīr*

2

Ibn Rushd (1126–1198)

In "There Is No Such Thing as Western Civilisation," Kwame Anthony Appiah (2016) deconstructs the signifiers "West" and "Western" as modern conceptions from the nineteenth century, which retroactively fabricate an ethnocultural European (i.e., "white") history with origins in the so-called Greek "miracle." Martin Bernal (1987), in *Black Athena*, calls this fabricated ethnocultural history "the Aryan Model," which he contrasts with the more accurate "Ancient Model" of the Classical and Hellenistic ages. The Aryan Model is not only false, according to Bernal; it is also racist: "Racism was, from the beginning, an important factor in the downplaying of the Egyptians and the dismissal of the Ancient Model, and after 1860 it became the overriding one" (p. 675). Conversely, the Ancient Model acknowledged the influence of Egyptians and Phoenicians on ancient Greece, therefore complexifying any essence of (non)Europeanness and opening up the third space of hybridity.

Accordingly, the history of philosophy is, in effect, a world history of (non) European philosophies; albeit European philosophy has fared better than Arab-Islamic philosophy for reasons I will explore. Chiefly among them was "the reluctance of the Muslim world, and the Ottoman Empire in particular, to embrace the printing press quickly enough" (Al-Khalili, 2010, pp. 763–4), which is ironic given that "the first ever book to be printed in England was the *Dictes and Sayings of the Philosophers* ... an English translation of an Arabic text" (p. 764). The printing press was not enthusiastically embraced in the Muslim world because printing "in Arabic type presented the early typesetters with far greater problems than Latin" (p. 764).

Consequently, the Muslim world reluctantly embraced the printing press in the seventeenth century, which accounts for the three-centuries-long epistemological gap between European and Arab-Islamic philosophies/ sciences, and it also speaks to the difference between European aesthetics and Arab poetics: "In the Islamic world, calligraphy was, and still is, far more than just an art form or an aesthetic style; it was a means of cultural identity" (pp. 765–6).

After all, Arabic is the sacred language of the Qur'ān and affords its speakers a modern poetic—and anachronic—sensibility. However, Arabic also can arrest the same speakers in traditional fantasies that fix *turāh* (heritage) as a thing of the past instead of an ongoing project of reviving poetic modernity. As such, whereas Europeans prefer futurism, Arabs are more comfortable with pastism; this distinction is a historical function of cultural—and colonial—difference and not an essentializing statement. These two ideals (i.e., futurism and pastism), which are obviously manifestations of the historical and theoretical tensions between science/philosophy and religion/theology, resulted in different subjectivities—modern and otherwise—that relate to temporality in distinct ways: linear and nonlinear, respectively.

Moroccan philosopher Mohammed Abdel al-Jabri critiques ideological pastism, wherein revivalism (*iḥyā'*) is essentially "religious traditionalism masquerading as modernism or reformism" (as cited in Fakhry, 2004, p. 373). For al-Jabri, this form of pastism "is the height of the unhistoricity of Arab-Islamic thought, or its inability to free itself from the clutches of the past" (p. 373). The renewal (*tajdīd*) of Arabic thought, according to al-Jabri, requires an epistemological break with tradition or heritage (*turāh*), which he views as an ideology that must be critiqued methodologically following the humanistic spirit of Ibn Rushd.

To the contrary, Adonis (1990) defends epistemological pastism, which he associates with poetic reason and artistic creativity: "We were split in two, our rational consciousness on the side of science and the future, and our hearts on the side of art and the past" (p. 94). Epistemological pastism entails invoking the timeless (or poetic) aspects of the past—for example, "legend, mysticism, magical and non-rational elements of the literary tradition, the mysterious regions of the human soul" (p. 95)—to strengthen our commitment to humanism in the present. Whereas *ideological pastists* have no issue marrying European modernization with their fundamentalist agenda, *epistemological pastists* resist the instrumental reason of both capitalists and fundamentalists in favor of historical/poetic reason, which prefigures a liberationist horizon: *al-madīna al-fāḍila* (the virtuous city) *qua* participatory democracy.

The originality of Ibn Rushd stems from his view that there is no contradiction between philosophy/science and theology/religion. The Averroists—the followers of Ibn Rushd in Europe and elsewhere—have named this position *double-truth theory*, wherein the truth is one even if the approaches to said truth are many. In other words, reason and faith are two valid epistêmês. "Although the history of philosophy has been described in terms of the dueling legacies of Plato and Aristotle" (Solomon & Higgins, 1996, p. 57), or rationalism versus empiricism, the Abrahamic religions introduce *revelation* as a third term excluded from this open-ended historical debate in the philosophy of science.

Modern scientists reject revelation and regard it as nonscientific or irrational; however, Ibn Rushd accepted revelation and approached the Islamic tradition through the lens of Peripatetic philosophy, particularly making use of *demonstrative logic as a methodology of allegorical interpretation*: "If the apparent meaning of Scripture conflicts with demonstrative conclusions it must be interpreted allegorically, i.e. metaphorically" (Ibn Rushd, 1179/2015, p. 50). Therefore, Ibn Rushd's approach represents an alternative to both scientistic and religious dogmatism. The modern scientist rejects revelation as unworthy of rational inquiry, and the religious fundamentalist accepts revelation literally, thereby bracketing poetic reason.

Having acknowledged the epistemological gap between European and Arab-Islamic philosophies/sciences, the development of European philosophy since the European Renaissance would not have been possible without Arab-Islamic philosophy's revival of ancient Greek philosophy during the European Middle Ages, which is also known as the Islamic Golden Age, as represented by first the Abbāsid Caliphate (Baghdad) and later al-Andalus (Córdoba).

Jim Al-Khalili (2010) qualifies the Islamic Golden Age as the age of "Arabic science" because Arabic back then was "the lingua franca of science in the medieval world" (p. 55), the way English is today. The age of Arabic science would not have been possible without the support of Abbāsid Caliphs, who funded a "massive translation movement—a process that lasted for two centuries—during which much of the wisdom of the earlier civilizations of the Greeks, Persians and Indians was translated into Arabic" (p. 170). This movement culminated in the building of a major Baghdad library, sponsored by Caliph al-Ma'mūn, known as the House of Wisdom (*bayt al-hikma*).

Most translations were done by "Christians of the Nestorian or Jacobite sect" (Fakhry, 2004, p. 16), who translated Greek philosophy first into Syriac and then into Arabic—this, for instance, shows the cosmopolitan potential of an enlightened Caliphate as a borderland space of radical copresence, wherein ecologies of knowledges are honored through intercultural translation. Ḥunain b. Isḥāq (809–873), along with "his son Isḥāq, his nephew Ḥubaish, and his disciple 'Īsā b. Yaḥia were responsible for translating almost the whole Aristotelian corpus" (p. 13).

The Arabs were interested in Greek philosophy—in addition to Persian and Indian philosophies—for both practical and theoretical reasons. Practically, there was a desire to learn about and apply Greek science (medicine, alchemy,

Figure 1 Ibn Rushd looking through a proto-telescope.
Source: Misr International Films.

and astrology). Theoretically, scholastic theologians (*mutakallimūn*) also needed the methodological tools of Greek philosophy (e.g., dialectics) to logically defend Islam against the naysayers. In addressing the lasting effect of Greek philosophy on the different schools of Islamic theology, Fakhry writes:

> The "Traditionism" of early theologians and jurists, such as Mālik b. Anas, was no longer tenable in its pure or original form. The great Ash'arite "reformers," committed as they were to the defense of orthodoxy against heretics and free thinkers, could no longer do so without recourse to the weapons which their rationalist opponents had borrowed from the Greeks. It was as though *the ghost of Greek dialectic could no longer be exorcised without recourse to the formula of exorcism which it had itself enunciated in the first place.* (p. xxii, emphasis added)

The history of Islamic philosophy can be summarized as an epistemological and ideological struggle between rationalists, mystics, and fundamentalists. The three groups interpret Islam through different forms of reasoning: the first group consists of the philosophers (e.g., Ibn Rushd) who use *al-burhan* (demonstration), the second group consists of the scholastic theologians (e.g., al-Ghazālī) who use *al-irfan* (dialectics), and the third group consists of the traditionists (e.g., Ibn Taymiyah) who use *al-bayan* (rhetoric).

Today, the third group (*Salafiyya*) has the loudest voice, particularly given the Saudi regime's support for the Wahhābī movement. Salafis idealize *al-salaf al-ṣāliḥ* (the pious ancestors) and consider nonliteral approaches to the Islamic tradition as *bidʿah* (heresy). The second group, which happens to be one of the most politically hegemonic today, is represented by modern Islamic reform movements (e.g., Al-Azhar in Egypt) and *Tasawwuf* (Sufism). Currently, the first group is politically speaking the weakest of all three, and it consists of the various intellectuals who draw on humanism, secularization, existentialism, and/or Marxism—that is, rationalist epistemologies—in their critiques of fundamentalist ideology.

Unlike Bertrand Russel (1945), who wrote in *A History of Western Philosophy* that "Arabic philosophy is not important as original thought" (p. 427), I will stress the originality of Ibn Rushd's postabyssal thinking. Ibn Rushd's border thinking ought to be qualified as postabyssal, for it was nonderivative thinking; to put it differently, he was not merely a "transmitter" of Aristotle. Rather, Ibn

Rushd drew on ecologies of knowledges (e.g., Aristotelianism and Islam) and enacted an intercultural translation between them.

Arab-Islamic philosophers translated, reinterpreted, commented on, and extended works of Greek philosophy and science, as al-Khalili (2010, p. 309) shows. Otherwise, why would al-Khwārizmi, whose name in Latin is Algorithmus, be considered the father of algebra? After all, "the word 'algebra' is derived from the book's title: *Kitab al-Jebr*" (p. 310). Or, why would Ibn Rushd be considered "the father of secular thought in Europe and one of the most important philosophers of all time" (p. 732)? Furthermore, Ibn Rushd, whom Fakhry (2004) dubs "the great Aristotelian of Islam" (p. 270), is the only Muslim philosopher represented in Raphael's (1509–11) famous fresco: The School of Athens. He had to be somewhat original to earn a place there; however, Euromodern recognition or validation of non-European poiēsis is not the main point of this book, for my primary target audience is the Other of the Other.

There is an assimilationist danger in the inclusion of Other-thought, such as Ibn Rushd's philosophy or Chahine's cinema, into the totality of the modern system as medieval philosophy or auteur cinema, respectively. From the perspective of transmodernity, intercultural translation ought to facilitate a dialogue between the different ecologies of knowledges without negating or erasing the Other's exteriority. What makes Ibn Rushd innovative is his synthesis of Aristotelian philosophy with Islam. Thus, affirming his Aristotelianism while bracketing the primacy of Islam for his border thinking and cosmopolitan being would be dishonest, to say the least.

During the era of Latin Scholasticism, Aristotle came to be known as the Master or the Philosopher, while Ibn Rushd was revered as the Commentator. Back then, medieval universities (e.g., the Universities of Paris, Oxford, Padua) were founded on a core curriculum that consisted primarily of texts by Aristotle and Ibn Rushd, read side by side. Ibn Rushd was widely translated from Arabic to Hebrew and Latin, which opened the door for Latin translations of Aristotle and other ancient Greek philosophers culminating in the European Renaissance in the fifteenth century, which I qualify as such to distinguish it from the later Arab Renaissance (*al-nahḍa*) that began in the late nineteenth century.

According to Hussam Ahmed (2021), in his book *The Last Nahdawi*, *al-nahḍa* "was first and foremost [an intercultural] translation project that translated not only English and French texts into Arabic but was also translating Arabic and Arab subjectivity itself in the process" (p. 17). The *al-nahḍa* project was "a period of intense intellectual activity animated by heated debates over rupture with and/or return to the cultural foundations of Arab-Islamic thought" (p. 28). One such heated debate was between Mohammed 'Abduh (Islamic reformist) and Farah Antun (secular humanist), revolving around the rationalist philosophy of Ibn Rushd and the question of secularizing Islam (cf. Najjar, 2004). *al-nahḍa*, therefore, was a short-lived pluriversal political project that embraced ecologies of knowledges. Unfortunately, the ideological monoculturalism of Arab nationalism would soon come to replace *al-nahḍa* project.

Stephen Sheehi (2004) comments, "While Antun never argued according to a race-based theory, clearly he and Abduh were debating whether or not the idea of progress and civilization—the cornerstones of modernity—is inherent to Arabo-Islamic culture" (p. 157). Furthermore, Ahmed (2021) adds that the two tasks of *al-nahḍa* were "reviving *adab* [literary] humanism and at the same time integrating the sophisticated accomplishments of western civilization" (p. 74, emphasis in original). But *al-nahḍa* was not without its critics, as Tarek el-Ariss (2013) shows: "For his part, Sadiq Jalal al-Azam (b. 1934) undertakes a Marxist critique of Arab society's blind embrace of *Nahda* liberation discourse without adequately scrutinizing traditional forms of authority and beliefs" (p. 4, emphasis in original). Consequently, historical reason, in the form of Arab poetics, must be the central scrutinizer responsible for self-criticism.

el-Ariss (2013) continues, "According to al-Azm, the 1967 Arab defeat against Israel, or *Naksa*, exposed the absence of this radical critique and exacerbated the discrepancy between the discourse on modernity and Arab social and political structures" (p. 4, emphasis in original). In a sense, *al-nahḍa* was a decolonial response to the French, British, and Ottoman colonization of the Arab world, which exacerbated the already tense relationship between modernity and its alterity; however, the liberationist project of *al-nahḍa*, which had a transmodern potential, was thwarted by a series of traumatic events from the *nakba* (catastrophe) of 1948 to the *naksa* (setback) of 1967.

These traumatic events, in Palestine and elsewhere in the Arab world, were further aggravated by the military modernization of the post-/neo-colonial world as funded, in particular, by the United States. Hence, the encouraged political response to these traumas, according to US foreign policy, has been their endocolonial repetition in the form of sub-oppressive authoritarianism.

Ibn Rushd was seen as a heretical figure not only by Muslim traditionalists but also by the Church authorities, which is a sign of the modernity of his thinking in light of Peter Berger's (1979) argument that *modernity is the universalization of heresy*. Fakhry (2001) writes, "In 1277, a papal bull was issued on which Etienne Tempier based his second condemnation of 219 theses directed against Averroes" (p. 135). The charge of Averroism stemmed from Ibn Rushd's emphasis on the "primacy and autonomy of reason" (p. 137) in the face of any form of dogmatic authority, Church or State.

Dogmatism, or fundamentalism, is often premised on a literalist and absolutist view of truth, which Ibn Rushd regarded as a form of rhetorical reasoning; on the other hand, rationalism, or secularization, involves the demonstrative method of interpretation, which requires syllogistic logic or deductive reasoning. Ibn Rushd was not the only heretic Muslim philosopher in history; the list also includes al-Kindī, al-Farābi, al-Rāzi, and Ibn Sīnā. The rationalist (philosophical/scientific) line of Islamic humanism, represented by these heretics, has unfortunately been historically defeated by both the mystical approach of al-Ghazālī—for example, Al Azhar in Egypt follows Ashʿarī theology—and the fundamentalist path of Ibn Taymiyyah, which is embodied today in the Wahhābī movement known as Salafiyya. Nevertheless, and despite the ultimate failure of both Islamic humanism and the Arab Renaissance, Arab Averroists do exist and include figures such as Farah Antun, Mohammed Arkoun, Mohammed ʿAbed al-Jabri, Nasr Abu Zayd, Majid Fakhry, Ziauddin Sardar, Youssef Ziedan, Monna Abousenna, Nawal El Saadawi, and Mourad Wahba (cf. von Kügelgen, 1996).

Hegemonic historical accounts following the Aryan model will credit René Descartes for inaugurating secular humanism as well as modern philosophy and subjectivity (e.g., Ferry, 2010, p. 127); however, if it were not for Ibn Rushd's philosophical rationalism along with its implicit secular humanism, Descartes's mathematical rationalism would not have been possible (Fakhry,

2001, p. 137). Majid Fakhry also adds that Ibn Rushd's philosophical rationalism was more "comprehensive" than the mathematical rationalism of Descartes (p. xvi), even though it precedes it by five centuries. In what follows, I will highlight the cosmopolitan importance of Ibn Rushd as a transmodern figure and the radical humanism of his rationalist philosophy, which crystallize some of the coordinates of historical reason: pluriversal politics, ethics of liberation, ecologies of knowledges, and decolonial poiēsis/aísthēsis. The former coordinates constitute a transmodern sociology of emergences, which must accompany any decolonial sociology of absences. As such, I must resume my critique of the ethnocentric approach to human civilization, for its negation of border thinking or Other-thought.

For Appiah (2016), "the very idea of the 'west,' to name a heritage and object of study, doesn't really emerge until the 1890s, during a heated era of imperialism, and gains broader currency only in the 20th century." He adds, "If the notion of Christendom was an artefact of a prolonged military struggle against Muslim forces [i.e., the Crusades], our modern concept of western culture largely took its present shape during the cold war." In other words, while the "west" may be defined positively in terms of "liberty, tolerance, and rational inquiry," it is often conceptualized in relation to its opposite: the non-Christian/non-European world. Instead of an ethnocentric notion of identity premised on false essentialism (European or otherwise), Appiah proposes *a cosmopolitan subjectivity grounded in radical humanism.*

Whereas radical humanism is truly universal, liberal humanism has the semblance of universality but is, in fact, ethnocentric, if not racist. Therefore, it is questionable whether we should continue to consider liberal humanism as a form of humanism. For Said (2004), humanism is "the secular notion that the historical world is made by men and women, and not by God" (p. 11), "the achievement of form by human will and agency" (p. 15), "critique that is directed at the state of affairs" (p. 22), and "a resistance to *idées reçues*" (p. 43, emphasis in original). Humanism, he continues, "is about reading, it is about perspective … it is about transitions from one realm, one area of human experience to another. It is also about the practice of identities other than those given by the flag or the national war of the moment" (p. 80). Consequently, the methodological impetus of "radical humanistic critique" (Said, 2004, p. 53) is textual interpretation, which was central for both Ibn Rushd and Chahine as border thinkers who honored ecologies of knowledges in their intercultural translations.

Philosophy began due to a rich cultural exchange between Mediterranean cultures (e.g., Egyptian, Phonecian, Greek). When we speak of ancient Greek philosophy, for example, we are referring to the thinking of various philosophers who lived in city-states that were later unified under the imperial rule of the Macedonians. The fact that they spoke the same language facilitated their critiques of *idées reçues*—a central characteristic of secular criticism *qua* radical humanism. Similarly, when we mention Arabic philosophy, we mean a philosophy communicated in Arabic (even if not necessarily by Arabs), which often staged an "inter-philosophical dialogue" (Dussel, 2009) between Greek philosophy and Islam regardless of the philosopher's religion or ethnicity.

In other words, cultural groups that speak the same language are never monolithic. Islamic philosophy, for instance, is a history of debates among Islamic philosophers who represented different philosophical or theological tendencies ranging from the sectarian, or political, distinction between Sunni and Shi'a, to the more nuanced differences between the major schools of Islamic jurisprudence within Islam. This Islamic history, which is in dialogue with the non-Muslim world, informs current political movements within Muslim-majority countries: Sufi, Salafi, humanist, or otherwise. I follow Mourad Wahba's (1995/2022) thesis that there is *one civilization with many cultures*; therefore, we should speak of (non)European cultures, particularly since "Europe" often signifies, albeit unconsciously, Western Europe.

Similarly, Arab-Islamic cultures refer to the twenty-two members of the Arab League, that is, countries where Arabic is an official language spoken by Arabs and non-Arabs. Since Arabic is the language of the Qur'ān, and given Islam's beginning in the Arabian peninsula, the Arab world is part of the Muslim world, but not vice versa, for the latter is a much broader category that is more diverse culturally—with India's 1.2 billion Muslim population being one prominent example.

As will become clear later on, cultural heterogeneity is one of the central features of Chahine's transmodern cinema, which renders it nonideological. Being Arab, for Chahine, is more than an ethnic designation; it is a political commitment to a pluriversal politics of anticolonialism or a geo-/body-politics of decolonial knowledge. Being Arab signifies an ontological identification with the poetics of Arab modernity. The Arabic language and Arab culture are exterior ecologies of knowledges, which make delinking and border thinking possible.

This does not mean, however, that everything about Arab (or any Other) culture is good, for the transmodern task entails subsuming the *positivity* of both totality and exteriority through the lens of liberation ethics. Therefore, the positivity of modernity and its alterity are those theories and practices that can be applied in praxis for the liberation of oppressed peoples around the world. In my view, Ibn Rushd's philosophy and Chahine's cinema are positive examples of Other-thought produced in the exterior context of Arab-Islamic cultures.

Ibn Rushd's Biography: A Decoloniality of Knowledge

Abū al-Walīd Muḥammad ibn Ahmad Ibn Rushd, or Averroes in Latin, was born in 1126 in Córdoba, al-Andalus, and died in 1198 in Marrakesh, Morocco (cf. Arnaldez, 2000; Leaman, 1988; Urvoy, 1991). As Fakhry (2001) writes, Ibn Rushd hails from "a prominent family of religious (Mālikī) judges and statesmen, and in the manner of his father and grandfather, who served as Mālikī judges of Cordova, the young Averroes studied jurisprudence [*fiqh*], Arabic, letters (*adab*), theology (*kalām*), philosophy and medicine at the hands of a number of teachers [e.g., Ibn Bājja and Ibn Ṭufayl]" (p. 1, emphasis in original).

In 1169, Ibn Ṭufayl, his close friend and the author of the first philosophical novel *Ḥayy ibn Yaqẓān*, introduced Ibn Rushd to the Almohad Caliph Abū Ya'qūb Yūsuf, who reigned from 1163 to 1184 and was well versed in philosophy. The meeting had two positive outcomes: (1) Ibn Rushd was appointed as religious judge (*qāḍī*) of Seville, and (2) he was tasked by the Caliph to comment upon Aristotle's works. The Caliph was interested in Aristotle's philosophy but found it too complex, which is why Ibn Ṭufayl recommended Ibn Rushd. In 1171, Ibn Rushd was promoted to chief *qāḍī* of

Figures 2–3 Ibn Rushd in *al-Maṣīr* (1997).
Source: Misr International Films.

Córdoba. Later, he was also appointed as the court physician of the Caliph. The Arabic title *al-ḥakīm* (the all-wise) was apt because the word captured the two functions of Muslim *falasifa*: philosopher and physician.

Ibn Rushd produced thirty-eight commentaries on Aristotle; by the thirteenth century, fifteen were already translated into Latin by pioneers, such as Michael the Scot and Hermann the German. Fakhry (2001) writes:

> When Averroes' commentaries on Aristotle were translated into Latin early in the thirteenth century, they caused a profound intellectual stir in philosophical and theological circles in Europe, and laid the groundwork for the rise of Latin Scholasticism ... Even the rise of Renaissance rationalism and humanism is closely linked to Averroes' commitment to the primacy of reason in philosophical and theological discourse. (p. xv)

Ibn Rushd wrote three types of commentaries: "large (*tafsīr*), intermediate (*sharh*) and short, i.e. paraphrase or epitomes (*jawāmiʿ*)" (p. 3, emphasis in original). Peter Adamson (2016) questions this common distinction: "More helpful would be to talk of epitomes and paraphrases, reserving the word 'commentaries' for the five massive works of exegesis [i.e., the *Posterior Analytics*, *On the Soul*, the *Physics*, *On the Heavens*, and the *Metaphysics*]" (p. 180).

Ibn Rushd wrote systematic commentaries on all works by Aristotle except *Politics*, which was not available in the *ummah* during that time. Ibn Rushd's impressive effort earned him the nickname "The Commentator" among Latin Scholastics. In addition to his erudite commentaries on Aristotle, Ibn Rushd also wrote several original philosophico-theological texts, such as *Tahāfut al-Tahāfut* (The Incoherence of the Incoherence), *Fasl al-Maqāl* (The Distinction of Discourse), and *Al-Kashf ʿan Manāhij al-Adillah* (The Exposition of the Methods of Proof). Fakhry (2004) writes:

> The three major parts of Ibn Rushd's work could be seen as his commentaries upon or interpretation of Aristotle, his criticism of al-Fārābi and Ibn Sīnā in the name of a pure Aristotelianism ... and his demonstration of the essential harmony between philosophy properly understood and Scripture properly interpreted. (p. 283)

Adamson (2016) believes that Ibn Rushd's approach was "a doubly outdated endeavor, an attempt to revive the Baghdad revival of late antique Alexandria"

(p. 181). Adamson continues, "For a post-Avicenna, post-Ghazālī audience of Muslim thinkers, Averroes' commentaries were the equivalent of silent films made after the invention of sound" (p. 182). I find this derogatory analogy unconvincing given that the history of European philosophy is essentially a debate between Plato and Aristotle; furthermore, poetic reason in Arab modernity follows anachronic temporality as opposed to the linear myth of "progress" associated with the coloniality of time.

In 1194, four years before his death, Caliph Abū Yūsuf al-Manṣūr "ordered his books to be burned and carted him off to Alisana (Lucena), a small town to the southeast of Cordova, together with other students of philosophy and science" (p. 282). There is no definitive account as to why this twist of fate befell Ibn Rushd; however, Fakhry postulates that it was "possibly in response to public pressure or due to a personal grudge" (pp. 281–2).

In a 2021 documentary in Arabic on Ibn Rushd produced by Al-Jazeera, Atef Aliraqi argues that Ibn Rushd was the last Arab philosopher. Aliraqi concedes that there are many *thinkers* in the Arab world today but no contemporary Arab-Islamic *philosophy*, which seems to be a case of colonized intellectualism since that disparaging distinction between philosophy and thought is an Orientalist feature of Euromodernity. Albert Hourani (1991) makes a similar argument when he writes, "The thought of Ibn Rushd was the final expression in Arabic of the philosophical spirit" (p. 190). Nevertheless, contemporary examples of Arab-Islamic philosophy in the spirit of Ibn Rushd include Mourad Wahba and Monna Abousenna's (1996) project on Ibn Rushd as an enlightening intercultural bridge (cf. Al Tamamy, 2014), Mohammed 'Abed al-Jabri's (1999, 2011) "critique of Arab reason," and Mohammed Arkoun's (2006) "critique of Islamic reason."

But why was Ibn Rushd more influential—at least, visibly so—in the history of European philosophy and somewhat absent in Arab-Islamic philosophy? According to Adamson (2016):

His failure to make an impact in the East could in part be thanks to the practical difficulties of copying such enormous texts and carrying them across such a large distance. In fact, it's generally true that Andalusian thinkers had little impact on the eastern tradition, unless they actually went east themselves, like the great mystical thinker Ibn 'Arabī. (p. 181)

Ernest Bloch (2019) qualifies Ibn Rushd, along with Ibn Sīnā, as part of what he terms the "Aristotelian Left" (p. 14). For Bloch, the Aristotelian Left naturalized *nous* and brought it down to earth. Bloch writes, "There is an increasingly predominant interest in the worldly" (p. 15), which echoes Said's humanistic arguments for worldliness in his essay on secular criticism. The Aristotelian Right (e.g., Thomas Aquinas), on the other hand, "elevated the concept of *nous* even further than Aristotle already had" (p. 16). The Aristotelian Left naturalized *nous* in three ways, according to Bloch: "*first*, the doctrine of *body and soul*; *second*, that of *active understanding or universal human intelligence*; and *third*, the *relationship between matter and form (potentiality-potency)* in the world" (p. 16, emphasis in original).

For Bloch, the main approach of the Aristotelian Left is "*the sublation of divine potency itself in the active potentiality of matter*" (pp. 15–16, emphasis in original). He adds, "The orientation of the Aristotelian Left emerges via the reconstruction of the matter-form relationship as one that clearly grasps matter as an active force—not just as something mechanically inert" (p. 23). Following Bloch, radicalism is materialist, and conservatism is idealist. Ibn Rushd's radicalism stems from his rationalist and humanist commitment to understanding how the world works in its material immanence. On the other hand, the conservative prefers living in the ideal world of pious ancestors while fantasizing about paradise: the transcendent world to come, not here on Earth but elsewhere. According to Bloch, the European Renaissance—and even Marxism—would not have been possible without the speculative materialist philosophy of the Aristotelian Left.

I wish to stretch Bloch's theorization by considering Chahine as a member of the Aristotelian Left, for he is a thespian of the Averroist variety. In addition to the biographical similarities between Ibn Rushd and Chahine as heretical border thinkers, the Blochian conception of the Aristotelian Left provides a theoretical link between both figures and their philosophical and aesthetic works, respectively.

Indeed, Chahine's radical films may be characterized as worldly or humanistic, particularly in light of the following remark given during an interview for Maspero TV in Egypt: "Through Alexandria, I can tell the story of a human being, as a member of humanity, and this is universality." Chahine's remark brings to mind Žižek's (2000) dialectical point about directly jumping "from the singular to the universal, bypassing the mid-level of particularity" (p. 239). As a worldly or humanistic filmmaker, Chahine was, in effect, a secular critic concerned with the sociopolitical ideologies of his time and their concrete material implications, such as the dialectical relationship between parasitic capitalism and religious fundamentalism, which has been plaguing the Arab world since the 1970s (cf. Wahba, 1995/2022).

Chahine's secular criticism comes full circle with his 1999 film *al-Akhar* (The Other), whose title references Said's (1978/2003) use of notion in *Orientalism*. The film, which follows *al-Maṣīr* and deals with the organic relationship between parasitic capitalism and Islamic fundamentalism in Egypt, features an appearance from Edward Said, in the first two minutes, playing himself. Said's speech to the film's protagonist (Adam) about the East versus West may be summarized using the Wahbian axiom: *one civilization, many cultures*. Said, like Wahba, rejects the false dichotomy of East versus West in favor of a worldly humanism grounded in cosmopolitan being and border thinking. Said's transmodern thesis would not be tenable without *a material reading of world history*, which is accomplished by historical reason.

Islamic Philosophy of Liberation

In their essay on decolonial aísthēsis, Walter Mignolo and Rolando Vázquez (2013) cite a passage from a short story by Jorge Luis Borges (1964) in his book *Labyrinths*. The story is titled "Averroes' Search." In the passage, Ibn Rushd has difficulty translating Aristotle's *Poetics*, particularly the words "tragedy" and "comedy." Borges writes, "No one in the whole world of Islam could conjecture what they mean" (p. 149). Mignolo and Vázquez interpret Ibn Rushd's difficulty in translating these two words as stemming "from the simple fact that the Greek concept of 'mimesis' was totally alien to Islam, and of which ... Islam has no need" (p. 9). They add, "Mimesis is not a universal concept" (p. 9).

However, according to José Miguel Puerta Vílchez (2017), Ibn Rushd did have a theory of mimesis, which restricted "poetics to Islamic ethics and logic"

(p. 322) and depended "more on resemblance to reality than on the imaginative reconstruction of reality" (p. 327). Puerta Vílchez continues, "Morally, poets may be of two kinds: those that move people toward good and those that move them toward evil" (p. 325). Peter Adamson (2022) also adds:

> The basic idea of Borges' story is that Averroes wouldn't have understood that Aristotle was describing a theatrical performance since, in Islamic culture, they instead had poetic recitation. This is probably true to a significant extent. Still, it should be borne in mind that there was undoubtedly mimetic poetry in Arabic, and the idea of imitation of action comes through very clearly in the Arabic version of *Poetics*. So if Averroes could not grasp what Aristotle was talking about, it would be more about things like not understanding actors on a stage, wearing masks, etc., and not about the idea of mimesis. (personal communication)

According to Mignolo and Vázquez (2013), "When aesthetics replaced poetics in eighteenth-century Europe … aesthetics was universalized and became used as a normative framework within European philosophy … to disdain or ignore the multiplicity of creative expressions in other societies" (p. 9). Indeed, Ibn Rushd was operating within the context of an Arab-Islamic poetic tradition characterized by *linguistic poiēsis* and *aniconic aísthēsis*; however, there is also a history of Arab aesthetics, which Puerta Vílchez (2017) captures succinctly in the following Prophetic saying: "Three things are radiant in our sight: a garden, running water, and a beautiful face" (p. 563).

Arabic, the language of the Qur'ān, is a sacred language. al-Qur'ān, which literally means the recitation, is a writerly text—a function of the complexity of the Arabic language and the figurative possibilities it affords to its speakers. Qur'ānic hermeneutics is a rich tradition, which Abousenna (1996) claims was founded by Ibn Rushd "through his theory of allegorical interpretation" (p. 107). Similarly, Nasr Abu Zayd (2004) writes, "A humanistic hermeneutics of the Qur'ān must take seriously the living phenomenon and stop reducing the Qur'ān to the status of *solely* a text" (p. 13, emphasis in original). In other words, given the association between mimêsis and idolatry in the Islamic tradition, most Muslim subjects (including Ibn Rushd) value a nonrepresentational, or aniconic, aísthēsis grounded in a linguistic poiēsis, which explains the hegemony of calligraphy in the Arab-Islamic world, for example, and the suspicion regarding the printing press, as mentioned before.

In a different essay, Walter Mignolo and Madina Tlostanova (2006) ask, "What then happened during the time span between Ibn-Rushd (1128–1198) who brought Muslim thought to its most rationalistic point and René Descartes?" and "why from Descartes onwards did the epistemic line erase Muslim contributions to human thought?" (p. 216). Their answer:

> Erasmus was one of the main agents in pushing Ibn Rushd out of the memory of a reconstituting Christian Spain, shortly after the final defeat of the Moors in 1492. And the point here is that there is a straight line between Erasmus' theology and Descartes' secular philosophy; while there is a profound gap between Erasmus and Descartes, on the one hand, and Al-Ghazali and Ibn-Rushd, on the other. A historical and epistemic gap was converted into a mirage and translated into a natural and logical historical continuity. The mirage is that it appears as if "universal history ... of thought" follows an ascending temporal line and, therefore, it is natural that René Descartes continued and took advantage of an accumulation of meaning that had been taking place in a genealogy that went from the Central-Asian philosopher and physician Ibn Sīnā ... to the Spanish Moroccan Ibn-Rushd. But that, as we all know, is not the way the history was told. Ibn-Rushd was eradicated from the universal march of human thought and Descartes—after Bacon—inscribed a genealogy of thought that was grounded in Galileo and in Aristotle; while Kant followed suit by replacing Galileo with Newton. To redress this history and to contribute to a pluriversal world in which many worlds can co-exist is one of the tasks of the border thinking and the de-colonial shift. (p. 216)

It is curious to think about what attracted Ibn Rushd and earlier Muslim philosophers to Aristotelianism given James Miller's (2011) characterization of Aristotle as "Faustian" (p. 111) and of Socrates as "ascetic" (p. 107). Like Faust, Aristotle made a devilish pact with the Macedonians—who were, as far as the Athenians were concerned, colonizers—offering his services as young Alexander's tutor for three years in exchange for unlimited power/knowledge. Even though Aristotle, who was from Stagira, was a student of Plato and an associate at the Academy for around twenty years, the position of scholarch after Plato's death did not go to Aristotle but to Plato's nephew

Speusippus. This drove Aristotle to start his school, the Lyceum, which rivaled the Academy.

The followers of Aristotle came to be known as Peripatetics because he was famous for philosophizing while walking through the Peripatos (walkway), and his students had to catch up with him and take notes. When Alexander the Great died, Aristotle was no longer welcome in Athens, so he was charged with impiety and exiled. Unlike Socrates, Aristotle did not wish to die for his ideas; he desired to live to contemplate everything. Consequently, Aristotle developed a philosophical system that spanned both the humanities and the sciences.

Furthermore, he invented the field of formal logic. The Muslim philosophers, beginning with al-Kindī, were very impressed with Aristotle's contributions to logic because it afforded them a scientific methodology for analyzing Scripture. However, no one mastered Aristotle like Ibn Rushd. Consequently, in his rebuttal to al-Ghazālī's *Tahāfut al-Falāsifah* (The Incoherence of the Philosophers), which was mainly a critique of al-Fārābi and Ibn Sīnā, Ibn Rushd argued that al-Fārābi and Ibn Sīnā were not true Peripatetics, for they read the Master through the distorting lens of Neoplatonism. Therefore, in his *Tahāfut al-Tahāfut*, Ibn Rushd engages in a double critique of Neoplatonism and Ash'arite theology (*kalām*).

The Averroist double-truth doctrine stems from Ibn Rushd's theorization of the three discourses used by the philosophers, the theologians, and the masses, which is not meant to signify a class hierarchy in an elitist Aristotelian fashion. Instead, the three discourses point to three methods of interpretation or three forms of reasoning. One can be described as philosophical or scientific, which is the demonstrative discourse. The other two (the dialectical discourse and the rhetorical discourse) are religious or theological. According to the double-truth doctrine, there is a single universal truth (e.g., humanism), which can be arrived at through different forms of reasoning, for "truth does not oppose truth" (Ibn Rushd, 1179/2015, p. 50). Rhetorical reasoning, which tends to be literal, aims to persuade the masses but does not arrive at the latent meanings of the Scripture.

Bassam Tibi (2012) asserts that Ibn Rushd's double-truth doctrine "paved the way for establishing modern rationalism" (p. 240); as such, he calls for "a revival of the grammar of Islamic humanism" (p. 241) as an alternative to Islamism or political Islam, which today tends to be fundamentalist, that is, absolutist or dogmatist. On the other hand, Islamic humanism (cf. Goodman, 2003, p. 24) signifies a unique cosmopolitan vision: a pluriversal politics based on Islamic ethics. To put it differently, it is the democratic application of what is true, just, and beautiful, according to Islam, to the realm of everyday life for the sake of collective liberation.

For instance, Chahine was not Muslim, and I am not Muslim, but we both grew up in a Muslim-majority country (Egypt) and, therefore, feel a special attachment to Islamicate culture. In other words, the pluriversal rationality of Islamic humanism (cf. Taylor, 2009) appeals to non-Muslims (e.g., Chahine and myself) as a function of its historical reason, which is often expressed poetically. Any human being can (and should) enjoy the magnificence of Islamic architecture and the brilliance of Islamic philosophy. As such, Islamic humanism is a potential source of inspiration, in Muslim-majority countries and beyond, for border thinkers interested in democratically developing an original secularization model delinked from the Christian-centric model prevalent in Euro-America. Wahba (1995/2022) defines secularization as "thinking of what is relative in relative terms and not in absolute terms" (p. 59). Therefore, secularization, as a process, entails distinguishing between the temporal and the spiritual without reducing one to the other as fundamentalism does: giving Caesar what is Caesar's and God what is God's.

Concretely, Islamic humanism is *the decolonial interpretation of the Arab-Islamic intellectual tradition to radicalize (i.e., pluriversalize) today's politics* (Daifallah, 2019). Patrick Williams (2014) argues that the Islamic humanism embodied by Ibn Rushd

> avoids many of the pitfalls of the version elaborated in the Enlightenment, not least through its inclusiveness. Chahine has said that one of the central aspects of his approach is "openness to the Other," and *that is precisely where Enlightenment humanism notoriously failed, in its inability to respond appropriately to its non-white, non-European Others.* (p. 87, emphasis added)

Dialectical reasoning—not to be confused with the Hegelian notion—produces an opinion (*fatwā*) through dialogue with individuals and through recourse to scholastic theology (*kalām*), oscillating between sophistry and logic. However, demonstrative reasoning treats poetical discourse as logical or scientific through deduction: syllogism or analogy (*qiyās*).

Following Aristotle, science for Ibn Rushd is knowledge of both the fact and the reason of the fact (i.e., causality). For example, Allāh, as pure form and actuality, is conceived as the final cause of all activity. The human is a material being whose essence and primary substance are formal—the psyche is the form of the body, and yet this form is a potentiality. We are driven teleologically toward the perfectly actualized form: *thought thinking itself.* Hence, according to Aristotle and Ibn Rushd, our ultimate destiny is the contemplative life: Other-thought or border thinking. This is the liberationist telos of historical reason: "If teleological study of the world is philosophy, and if the Law commands such a study, then the Law commands philosophy" (Ibn Rushd, 1179/2015, p. 44). The commanded love of wisdom is essentially a love of all forms of wisdom, modern or otherwise.

3

Youssef Chahine (1926–2008)

Before addressing Chahine's biography, I would like to situate his filmography within the contexts of (third) world cinema, minor cinema, African cinema, Arab cinema, and Egyptian cinema. As I have previously stated, the phrase "world cinema" is a metonym for "third-world cinema," which can be read as derogatory or complimentary.

(Third) World Cinema

In the derogatory sense, the third world implies developmental stuntedness in the Global South. This alleged underdevelopment is often framed in socioeconomic terms but also implies psycho-political deficiency; in other words, the Global South is framed as a developmentally stuck poor child. Furthermore, this would suggest that to be a third-world citizen is to be a third-class citizen. This meaning is rendered explicit during refugee crises, in particular, which raises the question of how Africa, as a metaphor for the Global South, is both the wealthiest continent in the world in terms of its natural resources *and* the poorest continent in the world in terms of its GDP per capita. This paradoxical situation is not accidental; it is an effect of the longue durée of the different forms of colonialism experienced on the continent since the fifteenth century: settler colonialism, franchise colonialism, and neocolonialism.

In the complimentary sense, the third world signifies solidarity toward a liberated world, or a *singularity-in-comradeship*, that is, a political project of nonalignment vis-à-vis the first world (laissez-faire capitalism) and the second world (state capitalism). Consequently, epistemologies of the South represent a Hegelian third term—the third space of hybridity—the possibility of an Other world negated by "cold" war ideology.

The reality of the (post)colonial world today can be characterized as more colonial than postcolonial. One of the reasons for this situation is the regression from anticolonial nationalism to cultural nationalism, which "emphasized racialism, religion, and hierarchy" (Prashad, 2007, pp. 163–4). This regression indicates a political shift from radicalism to conservatism, for, in contrast to cultural nationalism, anticolonial nationalism "drew from all sections of the oppressed population—men and women, working class and merchant—not only for demographic reasons but also because they had adopted the idea of equality" (p. 56).

Cultural nationalism, which characterizes politics in the (post)colonial world today, is undergirded by military modernization—a subfield created by Samuel P. Huntington (p. 140), who propagated the "clash of civilizations" myth. Military modernization, essentially a neoliberal strategy by the Pentagon, is the most concrete example of neocolonialism. The poster child of military modernization in the Global South is General Augusto Pinochet, who led a military coup in Chile, sponsored by the CIA, against the democratically elected socialist government of Salvador Allende.

This people's history is vital because, as represented by Gamal Abdel Nasser, Egypt was one of the leaders of the third world project, which, for a period of time, was both an ugly reality and a shared dream of a democracy to come: an ugly reality of political repression, and a republican dream of a modern Egypt liberated from all forms of oppression. The Egyptian revolution of 1952 actualized the republican dream through a military coup by the Free Officers, but it led to a (post)colonial nightmare: military dictatorship. The legacy of the police state in Egypt is typically attributed to the second president of Egypt (Nasser), who advocated for Arab socialism *qua* nationalism while imprisoning Egyptian communists. Therefore, third-world cinema is a charged phrase when considering the political ambivalence of third-worldism. Now I turn to conceptualize Chahine's transmodern cinema as minor cinema following Deleuze.

Minor Cinema

The concept of "minor cinema" is based on Gilles Deleuze and Félix Guattari's (1986) notion of "minor literature," which they created to account for Franz Kafka's style as an author. They write, "A minor literature doesn't come from a minor language [e.g., Hebrew]; it is rather that which a minority constructs within a major language [e.g., German]" (p. 16). They then go on to list the three characteristics of minor literature, which are also applicable to minor cinema:

> The first characteristic of minor literature in any case is that in it language is affected with a high coefficient of *deterritorialization* ... The second characteristic of minor literatures is that *everything in them is political* ... The third characteristic of minor literature is that in it *everything takes on a collective value*. (pp. 16–17, emphasis added)

In *Cinema 2: The Time-Image*, Deleuze (1989) distinguishes between major, or classical, cinema and minor, or modern political, cinema. Whereas "classical cinema constantly maintained this boundary which marked the correlation of the political and the private ... This is no longer the case in modern political cinema, where no boundary survives to provide a minimum distance or evolution" (p. 218). Deleuze adds that minor cinema is "no longer constituted on the basis of a possibility of evolution or revolution, like the classical cinema, but on impossibilities," such as the "double impossibility ... of forming a group *and* that of not forming a group" (p. 219, emphasis in original).

Next, Deleuze lists Chahine among the "best third world film-makers" and adds, "Third world cinema is *a cinema of minorities*, because the people exist only in the condition of minority, which is why they are missing" (p. 220, emphasis added). In minor or modern political cinema, the personal is political, and this is nowhere more obvious than in Chahine's transmodern cinema, notably his autobiographical Alexandria quartet: *Alexandria ... Why?* (*Iskandariyya ... leh?*, 1979), *An Egyptian Story* (*Haddouta Misriyya*, 1982), *Alexandria, Again and Forever* (*Iskandariyya, kaman wa kaman*, 1989), and *Alexandria ... New York* (2004).

Following Deleuze, these films can also be qualified as *autopoietic*: the political creation of I or the creation of I as political. According to Deleuze,

> In Chahine's work, the question "why" takes on a properly cinematographic value, just as much as the question "how" in Godard. "Why?" is the question of the inside, the question of the I: for, if the people are missing, if they are breaking up into minorities, it is I who am first of all a people. (p. 220)

Deleuze continues:

> "But why?" is also the question from the outside, the question of the world, the question of the people who, missing, invent themselves, who have a chance to invent themselves by asking the I the question that it asked them: Alexandria–I, I–Alexandria ... But is this I not the I of the third world intellectual ... who has to break with the condition of the colonized, but can do so only by going over to the colonizer's side, even if only aesthetically, through artistic influences. (p. 221)

Chahine's transmodern subjectivity (see Figures 4–7) embodied his minority status in Egypt; for example, while secular in practice, he was brought up in the Melkite Greek Catholic Church. Chahine's humanistic films may begin from this singular minority position, but they typically jump to the worldly level of the pluriversal: the African, the Arab, and the Egyptian. Audre Lorde is often quoted as saying, "The master's tools will never dismantle the master's house." But the master's tools, or the tools of classical cinema, can be reappropriated to create something else: a minor or modern political cinema that dreams of an Other world—a just world from the perspective of border filmmakers.

Like how Kafka used German (as opposed to Hebrew) to express himself and his literary ideas, Chahine used the tools of classical cinema, for he pursued his higher education in the United States and received funding from France throughout his filmmaking career. I suppose this book, and decolonial theorizing in general, can be considered a form of *minor scholarship*, which is not to say it is less important than "major" scholarship. Rather, this is an ethical point about both the place of minor scholarship in relation to the totality of Euromodernity and the radical exteriority of Other-thought. For example, I created decolonial film theory as a minority scholar and a border thinker, who wishes to delink, in their liberation praxis, from "major" (i.e.,

Youssef Chahine (1926–2008) 103

hegemonic) ways of being and thinking vis-à-vis cinema or film theory. The decolonial move then is to reappropriate the master's tools—the way the Arabs reappropriated Greek philosophy to build a house of wisdom—while delinking these modern tools from coloniality. Chahine reappropriated the modern tools of classical cinema in a decolonial way by delinking hysterical modernity from colonial mastery.

Chahine's personal/political cinema is impossible, for it presupposes an audience that needs to be invented; his republican dream is premised on a democratic politics of difference, or dissensus, that guarantees equality for minorities (Christians, Jews, gays, etc.). This impossibility of cultural (i.e., colonial) difference is central to any pluriversal politics within transmodernity: "the impossibility of not 'writing,' the impossibility of writing in the dominant language, the impossibility of writing differently" (Deleuze, 1989, p. 217). In *Alexandria … Why?*

> Chahine confronts the impossibility of cinematically speaking to the minorities of Egypt without the deterrritorialisation of the Egyptian population itself; equally challenging is the impossibility of producing a film that speaks in Arabic and accentuates the Alexandrian local cultures and yet addresses an international audience; the impossibility of utilising the Hollywood cinematic language and yet maintaining the imprint of Egyptian cinema or the impossibility of including all minorities in Egypt without risking the unanimity of national identity. (Abdul-Jabbar, 2015, p. 161)

Chahine applied intercultural translation in the face of these impossibilities in an effort to create a bridge not only between European and non-European cinemas but also within non-European cinemas. As such, Chahine's cinematic worldliness is a function of his cosmopolitan dialogues with Egyptian, Arab, African, and European spectators and beyond. Let us now turn to the place of Chahine's transmodern cinema within Africa.

African Cinema

I now situate Chahine's cinematic oeuvre in the context of what David Murphy and Patrick Williams (2007) call "postcolonial African cinema." This designation suggests that "cinema" (i.e., Euro-American cinema) is ipso facto colonial:

> The fact that cinema emerges at the high point of colonialist expansion, as a technological system becomes tied ever more closely to the West, and, above all, involves a reliance on capitalist relations of production, means that, far more than any other postcolonial cultural medium, it exists in an ideological, political and economic nexus whose effect is potentially deleterious. (p. 17)

Murphy and Williams assert, "African cinema was largely born in the context of the anticolonial struggle and its immediate aftermath" (p. 5). In the 1960s and 1970s, "African cinema was at the cutting edge of a politically and artistically radical 'Third Cinema,' which explicitly rejected the capitalist world order of the West" (p. 5). Murphy and Williams consider Egypt as the exception to the "precarious existence" of African cinema; Egypt is "the continent's oldest film industry, having begun production in the 1920s, and in its heyday it was a leading exporter of films throughout Africa and the Middle East" (p. 6).

Figures 4–7 Youssef Chahine.

Source: Misr International Films.

Murphy and Williams periodize African cinema using the categories of precolonial, colonial, and postcolonial. Whereas "precolonial" African cinema retroactively indexes the African oral traditions, including "the complex figure of the griot as storyteller" (p. 7), colonial "African" cinema "confirmed colonialist stereotypes about Africans and African culture among the cinemagoing populations of the West, and as such contributed towards the ideological justification of the colonial enterprise" (p. 11). This paradox is a function of the fact that "there are almost no anticolonial films contemporaneous with the period of decolonisation" (p. 12). However, Murphy and Williams note, "One exception to this is *Jamila al-Jaza'iriyaa* (*Jamila the Algerian*, 1958) by the Egyptian director Youssef Chahine" (p. 12). Murphy and Williams attribute this exception to not only "the existence of a full-scale cinema industry in Egypt" but also "the courage and independence of Chahine ... demonstrated by the fact that the film was promptly banned in Algeria, in France and (unofficially) in Egypt" (p. 13).

Murphy and Williams identify the three tasks of postcolonial African cinema: "the question of the nation; historical memory; and the vexed issue of African theory for African practices" (p. 14). For African filmmakers such as Chahine, "the nation (independent, committed to progressive values) remains the central—and as yet only partially realised—postcolonial project" (p. 15). In postcolonial African cinema, "the maintenance and recovery of historical memory" is "a method of combating the effects of colonial oppression" (p. 15).

In *Les Damnés de la Terre*, Frantz Fanon (1961/2004) showed that colonialism "turns its attention to the past of the colonized people and distorts it, disfigures it, and destroys it" to "demean history prior to colonization" (p. 149). This sheds light on the radicality of Chahine's historical films (e.g., *Jamila al-Jaza'iriyya*, 1958; *al-Nasir Salah al-Din*, 1963; *al-Asfour*, 1972; *Adieu Bonaparte*, 1985; *al-Mohager*, 1994; *al-Maṣīr*, 1997) as "postcolonial guardians of memory" (p. 16) or as histories of the present. Furthermore, Chahine's autobiographical films (i.e., the Alexandria quartet) are simultaneously historical films, wherein what is going on collectively in the nation is often mirrored structurally at the level of the psyche.

Postcolonial African cinema's final task is developing "an appropriately African theory for the analysis of African cultural practices" (p. 17), which, as Murphy and Williams caution, is not the simple rejection of European theories. Instead, as Said (1993) writes in *Culture and Imperialism*:

> The post-imperial writers of the Third World therefore *bear their past within them*—as scars of humiliating wounds, as instigation for *different practices*, as potentially *revised visions* of the past tending toward a postcolonial future, as urgently reinterpretable and *redeployable experiences*, in which the formerly silent native speaks and acts on territory reclaimed as part of a general movement of resistance, from the colonist. (p. 212, emphasis added)

Next, Murphy and Williams explore three theoretical issues that pertain to spectatorship in African cinema: (1) identification/alienation, (2) popularity, and (3) representation. They reject the classical notion in psychoanalytic film theory, which posits "the spectator as a 'dupe' of the process of cinematic 'illusion'" (p. 20). They equally problematize the Marxist solution to this "problem" of identification or ideological interpellation. In other words, alienation or distanciation, which is associated with Bertolt Brecht's epic theater, will not magically transform the false consciousness of the identified spectator into critical consciousness. Instead, Murphy and Williams "are arguing for a more sustained engagement with the ways in which African films work as narratives rather than simply focus on what they are about" (p. 21), such as how Chahine's worldly cinema, which "is constituted by radical discontinuities, non-sequential shifts and dispersed narrative structures" (p. 41), mirrors the political complexity of both the nation and his psyche.

Even though "African movies are often better known on the international film circuit than in Africa itself," Murphy and Williams claim that "in the African context, critics often oppose the notions of 'popular culture'—meaning a radical, consciousness-raising culture—and 'people's culture' [i.e., elite or folk culture]—a spontaneous, but often fundamentally conservative culture" (p. 22). In other words, popular African cinema is the cinema of the people, which is ironic since many popular African films in their home countries may be considered arthouse abroad. Murphy and Williams argue, "The non-Westen countries that have managed to create genuine film *industries* [e.g., Egypt]" follow "a very similar model, combining elements of local narrative tradition with melodrama and the visually spectacular" (p. 23, emphasis in original).

When it comes to the question of representation, Murphy and Williams write, "African cinema exists in a Western-dominated global system and its politics of representation must be understood within the full complexity of this situation" (p. 27). The politics of representing Africa is a twofold task, which entails: (1) a critique of the Orientalist cinematic representations of Africa and Africans and (2) a resistance to cultural imperialism through radical African aesthetics that embody "a complex web of representativity" (p. 26) as opposed to a monolithic "authentic" essence. Postcolonial African cinema, in other words, is the postcolonial cinema of singular African filmmakers (e.g., Ousmane Sembène, Abdellatif Kechiche, Jehane Noujaim); postcolonial—or, better, decolonial—African cinema amounts to a pluriversal politics of self-representation. In the words of Said (1994):

> The intellectual's representations, his or her articulations of a cause or idea to society, are not meant primarily to fortify ego or celebrate status ... Intellectual representations are the *activity itself*, dependent on a kind of consciousness that is skeptical, engaged, unremittingly devoted to rational investigation and moral judgment. (p. 64, emphasis in original)

For Murphy and Williams, Chahine is the primary example of a postcolonial African filmmaker, a modern intellectual in Said's sense. They compare Chahine to C. P. Cavafy (as described by E. M. Forster):

> Never straightforward, never predictable, never one to toe the party line either in his political beliefs or in his approach to filmmaking, the difference constituted by his "slight angle" to social taboos, political positions and cinematic norms alike is perhaps his most distinctive feature. (p. 30)

Chahine's "slight angle to reality" is grounded in his singularity of being "a Lebanese Greek Christian in an Arab Muslim nation" (p. 30), which affords him an oblique perspective on things. The singularity/pluriversality of Chahine's cinematic worldliness, particularly in light of his minority status in Egypt, leads Deleuze to consider his films to be exemplary of minor or modern political cinema, as previously mentioned. This goes to show the heterogeneity of exteriority, wherein border thinking or Other-thought signify ecologies of

110   *Transmodern Cinema and Decolonial Film Theory*

knowledges as opposed to a monolithic Otherness as the Orientalists would have us believe. Murphy and Williams write, "Chahine's departure from cinematic norms was considered simultaneously excessive [for Egyptian spectators] and insufficient [for Western critics]" (p. 32).

Chahine's unconventional style as a border filmmaker, along with his focus on taboo subjects as a modern intellectual, often led to controversy. For example, the Egyptian censors banned a number of his films, namely *Jamila al-Jaza'iriyya* (1958), *al-Asfour* (1972), and *al-Mohager* (1994). All three films were considered too traumatic for different reasons. In the case of the revolutionary Jamila Bouhired, the French government considered her a terrorist, and the Algerian government considered her a traitor, so Chahine's biopic was banned in both countries. While it was never officially banned in Egypt, it was not screened in the country for several years. The film was successful, however, in the Soviet Union, and Chahine "was awarded the major prize at the 1959 Moscow Film Festival" (p. 32).

The case of *al-Asfour* is interesting, as Murphy and Williams recount: "The irony here, however, is that it is Chahine's powerfully pro-Egyptian and pro-Nasser film *Al-Asfour* (The Sparrow, 1972) which is subject to the arbitrary decisions of the censors" (p. 36, emphasis in original). Chahine's sardonic comment on the banning of *al-Asfour* was: "With the censors, nothing is ever clear or straightforward. They are bureaucrats, but who are they? Complete idiots. I know that, because the person in charge of censorship used to be one of my students" (as cited in Murphy & Williams, 2007, p. 36). In his later years, Chahine was not afraid to speak out against the Egyptian government because he felt immune due to his old age and prestigious status as the most prolific filmmaker in the country's history.

Regarding *al-Mohager*, Chahine was "put on trial for blasphemy, notionally for having dared to represent one of Islam's prophets [i.e., Joseph] on the cinema screen" (p. 32). Chahine was acquitted, but the experience left a bitter taste in his mouth, particularly in the context of a generalized depoliticization of Egyptian secular society in the face of Islamic fundamentalism. On October 14, 1994—the year of *al-Mohager*'s release—Chahine's close friend and Nobel Prize laureate Naguib Mahfouz was stabbed in the neck several times by a fundamentalist who was offended by the "blasphemous" novel

Awlad Haretna (Children of Our Alley, 1959), which, of course, he did not even bother to read.

Murphy and Williams relate that Chahine "was angry at the lack of response to the near-fatal attack on his friend" (p. 37). Chahine said, "There should have been thousands of us intellectuals up in arms, but it was a real problem getting any of them to protest. A lot of them are held back by fear" (as cited in Murphy & Williams, 2007, p. 37). On the role of the artist, Chahine remarked:

> You must participate. You can't be an artist if you don't know the social, political, and the economic context. If you talk about the Egyptian people, you must know about their problems. Either you are *with modernity* or you don't know what the hell you are doing. (p. 37, emphasis added)

Being with modernity, for Chahine, means championing the liberatory cause of historical reason, which for him took the humanistic form of a *radical politicization of film aesthetics*. Murphy and Williams describe Chahine's radical aesthetics in terms of his "tenacious advocacy of a set of beliefs grounded in humanism, secularism, tolerance, rationality, and an appreciation of culture in all its richness and variety" (p. 33). Chahine's radical politicization of film aesthetics is a transmodern/decolonial effort because it is essentially an ethico-political dialogue between totality and exteriority, which aesthetically delinks modernity from coloniality.

Similarly, in *The Story of Film*, Mark Cousins considers Chahine one of the most "rebellious" filmmakers. A concrete example of Chahine's radical aesthetics is *Adieu Bonaparte* (1985). As Said (1978/2003) shows, Orientalism, a Eurocentric field dedicated to distorting the Orient, became possible after Napoleon invaded Egypt in 1798 and especially after the publication of *La Description de l'Égypte* (1809–22). As such, Murphy and Williams qualify "Chahine's panoramic survey of his country [i.e., *Adieu Bonaparte*] as a *counter-Description* of Egypt, as a fledgling *anti-Orientalism*" (p. 38, emphasis added).

Chahine's political radicalism, as embodied in his transmodern/decolonial aesthetics, is grounded in Levinasian ethics: "Regarding his 1997 film *Destiny*, [Chahine] said that the character Ibn Rushd (Averroes) embodied what he himself had always advocated, namely 'openness towards the Other'" (p. 42).

In *al-Akhar* (The Other, 1999), Chahine deconstructs the false dichotomy of us versus them, which ideologically sustains the myth of a "clash of civilizations" between the West and the rest, by shedding light on the cultural or local manifestation of that myth in Egyptian society.

al-Akhar is a secular critique of the dialectical relationship between parasitic capitalism and Islamic fundamentalism in Egypt. On the surface, these societal forces may seem to be antagonistic. However, in reality, working-class Egyptians (*les damnés de la terre*) are the excluded Other, for they are not benefiting from the death-driven dialectic of capitalism-fundamentalism, which is a local manifestation of the global racial capitalist apparatus that is framed in terms of a "clash of civilizations."

Huntington's (1993) thesis falls apart immediately when one considers, for example, US support for *al-mujahideen* in the 1980s as a cold war strategy against the Soviet Union in Afghanistan. To put it differently, it would have been more accurate, before 1991, to speak of a clash of fantasies: capitalism versus communism—even though the latter was, in reality, state capitalism. It is true that Islamism, particularly since the collapse of the Soviet Union, has replaced communism as the new official enemy of the United States; however, Islamism is not a civilization, which led Said (2001) to speak of a clash of "ignorance."

It is worth repeating the Wahbian maxim (*one civilization, many cultures*), for it sheds light on the ongoing struggle between instrumental reason/oppressive modernization and historical reason/liberatory modernity. Whereas the ethos of oppressive modernization is liberal humanism or conservative antihumanism, *the democratic spirit of liberatory modernity is radical humanism* (cf. Said, 2004, p. 5). Therefore, we can speak of *a clash of (anti)humanist fantasies*, which Wahba (1995/2022) qualifies as a struggle between fundamentalism and secularization. Secularization is a humanist fantasy about a democracy to come: a pluriversal politics grounded in a transmodern system. Chahine's transmodern cinema is sustained by such a humanist fantasy.

Openness towards the Other (cf. Shafik, 2015) is represented in Chahine's transmodern cinema as a radical openness towards workers, Jews, gays, and so on. The question of the Other unravels the impossibility of being a nation, for Otherness is a structural necessity in any democratic politics of difference premised on dissensus among equal citizens. Murphy and Williams (2007) describe an anecdote involving Chahine and philosopher Alain Touraine, which underlines the filmmaker's humanistic philosophy and joie de vivre.

In a television program, Chahine asks Touraine, "Do you dance?" Touraine is confused by the question. Chahine resumes, "I can't imagine a philosopher who talks about happiness and doesn't dance ... dancing creates happiness." This bacchanal ethic is most visibly embodied by Chahine (via his character Yehia) in his third autobiographical film, *Iskandaria, kaman wa kaman* (Alexandria: Again and Forever, 1990), which Richard Brody (2020) considers a "masterpiece hiding on Netflix."

Laura Finke and Martin Shichtman (2015) point to the significance of Chahine's "coupling of philosophy with song and dance" in *al-Maṣīr*, which "works to contest oppressive state and religious power" through a celebration of the pluriversal politics of *convivencia* (coexistence)—a geo-/body-politics of radical copresence. For Ibn Rushd, *convivencia* is achieved primarily through historical/poetic reason (cf. Habti, 2011). Finke and Shichtman add that in the borderland space of al-Andalus, "philosophy is realized as music" because "music is a vehicle for knowledge more valuable than academic authority or political power, more precious than religion," which speaks to the poetic sensibility of historical reason, wherein epistemology is folded into aesthetics.

According to Don Hoffman (2007), "Chahine's functional use of Gregorian chant, Sufi hymns, and gypsy dances serves both to entertain and to underscore thematic oppositions and to destabilize the Otherness of the Other, as unfamiliar tonalities come to be the norm" (p. 34). In Chahine's words, "Music is the opposite of arrogance. It is a form of sharing. Everyone loves to sing and dance. It is always possible to say important things without boring one's audience, and even to give them pleasure in the process" (as cited in Fargeon, 1997, p. 48).

Murphy and Williams (2007) point out that Chahine's life-affirming philosophy, which has Nietzschean undertones, echoes the thinking of anarchist activist Emma Goldman, "If I can't dance, I won't join in your revolution." Therefore, the liberation ethics of Chahine's politicized aesthetics

Figure 8 Abdallah dancing with Manuella.
Source: Misr International Films.

entails not only openness toward the Other but also *dancing with the Other*; Chahine's love for life, his affirmation of the Other's radical exteriority, and his vision of a politics of difference coalesce and produce *a life-affirming aesthetic sensibility that celebrates a love for aesthetics* (i.e., meta-aesthetics).

This meta-aesthetics crystallizes most clearly in his autobiographical films, particularly *Iskandaria ... leh?* (Alexandria ... Why?, 1978), where his love for literature, drama, and cinema is foregrounded. Mohamed Khan (1969) considered Chahine—alongside Salah Abu Saif and Hussein Kamal—to be one of three "outstanding" Egyptian filmmakers; he wrote, "*His love for the cinema was inspired by a desire to paint with a camera*" (p. 50, emphasis added). Therefore, for Khan, Chahine is less a conventional dramatist and more an eccentric painter of film; a technical master whose "films are dependent on the visual, poetically composed and at times hauntingly effective" (p. 51). But technical mastery is ultimately less important than being a radical visionary when it comes to transmodern cinema.

Chahine's pluriversal politics of difference can be seen throughout *Iskandaria … leh*? First, in the relationship between Sarah and Ibrahim: "She is Jewish and upper-class; he is Muslim and working-class" (Murphy & Williams, 2007, p. 43), but their membership in a communist group unites them. Pluriversality can also be glimpsed from the gay relationship between Adel and Tommy, who are supposed to be enemies, but Chahine believes love conquers all. Having considered Chahine's cinematic worldliness vis-à-vis African cinema, I shall turn presently to an exposition of Arab cinema.

Arab Cinema

I would like to begin by considering Chahine's filmography in the context of Arab cinema, but I do not wish for the reader to think that Arab cinema is reducible to Egyptian cinema or even that Egyptian cinema is reducible to Chahine. This is far from the truth, for the cinemas of Algeria, Tunisia, Syria, and Palestine, for example, demonstrate with aesthetic force the transmodern/decolonial vision of radical Arab cinema, which was certainly influenced by European film movements (e.g., Italian neorealism, Soviet montage cinema, French *nouvelle vague*), but also managed to create a singular cinematic language undergirded by a political commitment to decolonization, particularly in the contexts of *al-nakba* (catastrophe) of 1948 and *al-naksa* (setback) of 1967.

Consequently, the Palestinian struggle is often the backdrop of Arab cinema, whether this ongoing struggle for liberation is represented directly on film, such as in the films of Elia Suleiman and Hany Abu-Assad, or not. In the words of Ussama Makdisi (2023), Palestine is an index of "anti-colonial Arabism" and the crystallization of "a deliberate decolonial affiliation." As such, *being Arab—in the most radical sense—signifies a political commitment to decolonial liberation*, which for me (as it was for Said and Chahine) takes the form of pluriversal politics, such as a binational Israeli-Palestinian state, a democracy to come, where Israeli and Palestinian citizens would have equal rights.

The list of important books on Arab cinema includes *New Voices in Arab cinema* (Armes, 2015), *Arab Cinema Travels* (Dickinson, 2016), *Studies in the Arab Theater and Cinema* (Landau, 2016), *Arab Film and Video Manifestos* (Dickinson, 2018), *Roots of the New Arab Film* (Armes, 2018), *The Cinema of Muhammad Malas* (Alkassim & Andary, 2018), *Arab Modernism as World Cinema* (Limbrick, 2020), *Cinema and the Algerian War of Independence* (Bedjaoui, 2020), *Cinema of the Arab World* (Ginsberg & Lippard, 2020), *Barra and Zaman* (Rakha, 2021), *Films of Arab Loutfi and Heiny Srour* (2021), *Cinema in the Arab World* (Elsaket, Biltereyst, & Meers, 2023), and *From Outlaw to Rebel* (Belkaïd, 2023).

My interest, as a decolonial film theorist, is not in the Orientalist representations of Arab characters in Euro-America cinema (cf. Shaheen, 2001); rather, I am curious about the cinematic self-representations of Arab filmmakers whose radical films leap from the singular to the pluriversal. The authoritative text on Arab cinema for me is Viola Shafik's (1998/2017) *Arab Cinema: History and Cultural Identity*. I am probably biased because I took a film course with Shafik at the American University Cairo during my undergraduate years. Shafik distinguishes between national identity—or "the role and effect of nationalism and national liberation movements on Arab cinema" (p. 3)—and cultural identity, which is a formal question that has to do with the artistic roots of Arab cinema in "Arab-Muslim culture and what are known as traditional or native arts [e.g., poetry, literature, oral narration, shadow play, theater, decorative ornaments, calligraphy, and traditional Arabic music or *tarab*]" (p. 4).

For Shafiq, culture is not about purity or authenticity but *hybridity* because "authenticity can only exist within an impermeable cultural environment, cut off from foreign influences" (p. 6). Indeed, transmodernity, as a third space beyond modernity and antimodernity, is hybrid. She regards nationalism and fundamentalism as "movements of purification" (p. 6), which are more ideologically regressive than materially progressive. Additionally, Shafik conceptualizes the cultural identity of Arab cinema in terms of the major genres that characterize films produced during the colonial and postcolonial periods.

During the colonial period, Arab cinema—that is, Egyptian cinema, since Egypt was "the only Arab country able to develop a national film industry during the colonial period" (p. 11)—manifested in the form of musical, melodrama, or farce. However, postcolonial Arab cinema can be described with other genres, such as literary adaptation, realism, history, and *cinéma d'auteur*. Shafik divides the postcolonial period into two distinct phases: before and after *al-naksa* (setback) of 1967. Realism, particularly socialist realism, was the postcolonial aesthetic form par excellence of Arab nationalism before June 5, 1967—when Israel defeated Egypt, Syria, and Jordan in the Six-Day War. In Chahine's words:

> No doubt, June 5 [the Six Day War] has contributed strongly to my awareness of the artist's responsibility toward society. Yet, to be honest, already after the revolution in 1952 I became aware of that responsibility—though in an abstract and diffuse way—when I found myself given a choice between participating in the events of reality that surround me or being content to observe them. This was maybe expressed in *Mortal Revenge* [Siraa fil-Wadi, 1954]. After June 5 I started changing: first I moved from bourgeois entertaining cinema by addressing certain topics within that cinema and started then to make films that correspond to society's needs. You have to produce films that are indispensable. (as cited in Shafik, 2016, p. 192)

After 1967, Shafik documents a clear shift in the postcolonial aesthetics of Arab cinema from realism to New Arab Cinema, which ranges "from observant portrayals of social conditions to autobiographical stories and avant-garde art movies. In contrast to commercial or socialist cinema, some currents of the New Cinema employ unconventional stylistic forms and transgress taboos" (p. 37). This aesthetic shift, which accompanied the political shift in consciousness following the Arabs' collective sense of defeat, opened the possibility for a transmodern/decolonial aesthetic beyond nationalism and toward internationalism.

New Arab Cinema entailed a delinking from both colonial and postcolonial cinematic aesthetics. In colonial "Arab" cinema, the Arab subject was either unrepresented (absent) or misrepresented (exoticized) through the distorting lens of Orientalism. In postcolonial Arab nationalist cinema, he or she was idealized and rendered into an ideological fantasy figure to the detriment of many ethnic and religious minorities. In transmodern/decolonial art cinema, the Arab is positioned as a complex subject constrained by the failure of nationalism *qua* pan-Arabism and the horror of authoritarianism *qua* militarism and fundamentalism. Shafik adds:

> The essentially new in Arab *cinéma d'auteur* is, unlike other forms of committed cinema such as realism, the radical striving for personal expression, be it on the aesthetic and formal level, or with regard to content. Also innovative is its dissociation from global political messages and ostensibly objective analyses. (p. 185)

Chahine's impressive filmography from 1950 to 2007 exemplifies the two main phases (and genres) of postcolonial Arab cinema: realism and auteur. Shafik (p. 189) credits Chahine for introducing the autobiographical film as a subgenre in New Arab (auteur) Cinema with his *Iskandaria ... leh* (Alexandria ... Why?, 1978), and considers him a stylistic "pioneer" for creating "his own individual style" (p. 98) since *al-Asfour* (The Sparrow, 1972)—which deals directly with the setback of 1967 and was subsequently banned for two years by the Egyptian censors. Chahine's success in creating a unique filmmaking style is, to a large extent, a function of his financial independence since 1972, when he established his own production company Misr International Films, which relied on foreign funding from Algeria, Lebanon, Germany, and, most significantly, France since the mid-1980s.

Shafik writes, "The explicit political statements Chahine made in his first two autobiographical films [i.e., *Alexandria ... Why?* and *An Egyptian Story*] fit partly into the anti-colonial discourse prevalent during this period" (p. 191). But even some of Chahine's realist films, such as *al-Ard* (The Land, 1969), exhibit a strong anticolonial spirit. *al-Ard*, which is perhaps Chahine's most Marxist film, "deals with the [class] struggle of small farmers against the tyranny of the big landowners" (p. 137). The film's actions take place during the 1930s—that is, after the formal independence of Egypt from Britain in 1922 but before real independence as such in 1952. Consequently, the film is a materialist critique of Ottoman capitalism as sustained by British colonialism.

Shafik introduces the Arabic concept of *iltizam* or "sociopolitical commitment and responsibility" (p. 155) to account for the anticolonial dimension of radical Arab cinema. Ibrahim Fawal (2001) similarly writes, "One of the most loyal adherents to the principle of *al-iltizam* is Youssef Chahine: a poet and thinker who happens to write his novels on the screen rather than the page" (p. 7, emphasis in original). Shafik sees the legacy of *iltizam* at work in "Chahine's attachment to political allegories" (p. 191), especially in his autobiographical films, which formally serve as disruptive counterpoints to the narrative, hence resulting in nonlinear plots as a function of their anachronic temporality.

Shafik highlights Chahine's *al-Nasir Salah al-Din* (Saladin, 1963) as a historical film, which, in effect, was a political allegory of the present. This is certainly the case with all of Chahine's historical films, including *al-Maṣīr*, but the literalism of the allegorical reaches its zenith with the following example:

> The parallel drawn between the medieval hero Saladin and Nasser (Gamal 'Abd al-*Nasir*), the ultimate idol of the unifying pre-independence Pan-Arabism, is already apparent in the film's title, "*al-Nasir* Salah al-Din [the Victorious Saladin]." The struggle of the Arab prince (who was in fact of Kurdish origin) against the crusaders is equated with the relationship of the contemporary so-called Arab world to expansionist Europe. Saladin appears in an extraordinarily positive light. He does not fight back the invaders by military superiority alone but also by virtue of his justice and cleverness. (pp. 169–70, emphasis in original)

Shafik's hesitant expression "so-called Arab world" stems from how she begins her book:

> The Arab world is not, as is often perceived, a monolith … The majority of its inhabitants adhere to Islam, but other religions are represented in the region, including Judaism, Christianity, and Islamic sects such as those of the Alawites and Druze. On the linguistic level little unity exists; in addition to the languages of ethnic minorities like Berbers, Nubians, and Kurds, the Arabic language itself has split into a huge variety of local dialects. (p. 1)

In other words, the Arab world is a necessary fiction, that is, an imagined community of Arabic speakers, primarily in North Africa and West Asia, many of whom (but not all) are Arabs and/or Muslims. Indexing an expression from Egyptian film critic Samir Farid, Mohammad Salama (2018) writes about how the "second renaissance of Egyptian cinema" in the 1950s "was soon pressed into the service of forming a modern Egyptian identity" (p. 166) grounded in "secular Arab nationalism" (p. 171), which was both anti-Islamist and anticolonial. Salama hones in specifically on Chahine's *Jamila al-Jaza'iriyya* (Jamila the Algerian, 1958) as a case study of "a marketable commodity for a secular, woman-empowering, de-Islamicized Egypt" (p. 177). Chahine does not shy away from stating where he stands politically, "I was born a socialist, I was born poor" (as cited in Salama, 2018, p. 200).

However, his rebellious spirit drove him to also be critical of Nasserism, "The revolution took place. But I did not agree with all the changes that it instituted: Nasser nationalized film. They replaced the expert with an officer. It was a matter of military socialism" (p. 200). He continues, "It is true I got angry with the group that surrounded Nasser; he had become totally fascist at certain times" (p. 202). Chahine never accepted being a propaganda tool of any Egyptian government: socialist or otherwise. Salama concludes, "Nasser rid Egypt of the overt power of the Muslim Brotherhood by forcing them to go underground, if only temporarily. But in the process of de-Islamicizing postcolonial Egypt, Nasser ... set out on a precipitous course of nationalism and military absolutism" (p. 189).

Bearing in mind the authoritarianism of both secular nationalism and Islamic fundamentalism, the decolonial option is to speak of *many Arab worlds and cinemas* as opposed to one Arab world and cinema; however, Shafik concedes that "a common topography" and "a comparable history regarding colonialism and dependency on foreign powers" (p. 1) constitute a social link between the majority of Arab countries. With that said, one must account for the hegemony of the Egyptian film industry in the Arab world, which Shafik attributes to the specificity of modern Egyptian history and culture:

> Egypt had a dynamic multicultural life in which native Egyptians always played an important role, and which remained relatively undisturbed by colonial authorities. Particularly after the national upheavals of 1919, native Egyptians developed a stronger interest in the medium [of cinema] and combined it with well established arts like popular musical theater... Beginning in the 1920s, nationalist-oriented entrepreneurs led by Talaat

Harb, founder of the Misr Bank, worked to develop an independent national industry. In 1925 Talaat Harb decided that cinema was a good investment opportunity and established the *Sharikat Misr li-l-Sinima wa-l-Tamthil* (Misr Company for Cinema and Performance), which was intended to produce advertising and information films. In 1934 he built the Misr Studio, which was inaugurated a year later. (pp. 12–14)

Consequently, the Egyptian film industry was a model to be imitated elsewhere in the Arab world by Lebanon, Syria, and Iraq (p. 2). Furthermore, "The continuous consumption of Egyptian mass production caused the audience in many regions to acquire at least a passive knowledge of the Egyptian dialect" (p. 27). This is a good place to switch gears and focus on Egyptian cinema and Chahine's place within it (cf. Armes, 1981).

Egyptian Cinema

Even though cinema was introduced to Egypt through Alexandria in 1986 (i.e., a year after its invention by the Lumière Brothers), the Egyptian film industry began properly in 1935 with Tal'at Harb's establishment of Studio Misr. Shafik writes:

> By 1948 six further studios had been built and a total of 345 full-length features produced. In the years after World War II, cinema was the most profitable industrial sector after the textile industry. Between 1945 and 1952 Egyptian production reached an average of 48 films per year, a number comparable to today's production. (p. 12)

She continues:

> In 1959, the Ministry of Culture established the Higher Film Institute that still provides the country with the necessary young professionals, be they technicians, set designers, scriptwriters, or directors. Almost all Egyptian directors [including my father] who started working after 1959 have graduated from this school. Together with the limits set by a commercial and industrial orientation, the Film Institute is responsible for the relative homogeneity and continuity of Egyptian film making, both in form and content. (pp. 23–4)

Before Tal'at Harb, one must mention Muhammad Bayyumi, whom Fawal (2001) calls "the pioneer of Egyptian cinema" (p. 10) with his establishment of Amun Films (the first Egyptian film studio in the 1920s). Bayyumi's 1923 short documentary about the return from exile of nationalist hero Sa'd Zaghloul is considered the first Egyptian film. One must also refer to two other pioneering films: *Qublah fil-Sahra* (A Kiss in the Desert) by the Lama brothers—two Palestinians born and raised in Chile—and *Laila* (1927). Fawal writes that *Laila*, in particular, is significant for three reasons: (1) "it was produced by a woman [Aziza Amir] in her early twenties," (2) "Aziza Amir was among three women to enter Egyptian film production," and (3) "*Laila* touches on the problematic relationship between East and West, a subject that preoccupies writers up till the present" (p. 12).

However, Fawal argues that *Zainab* (1930) is the "most important silent film ... directed by Muhammad Karim who would be enshrined in an Egyptian film pantheon had there been one" (p. 12). Karim was mentored by Fritz Lang and called himself "a graduate of *Metropolis*" (p. 13). Another pioneer of Egyptian cinema, Youssef Wahbi, founded Studio Ramses, "the first small studio in Egypt" (p. 5), and produced *Zainab*.

Karim, however, established a song-and-dance genre in Egyptian cinema that has been repeated ever since by many filmmakers, including Chahine: "melodramas with singing interludes" (p. 15), where the Egyptian *ughniya* (song) takes center stage in a form distinct from Hollywood musicals: "The Egyptian musical genre remains a hybrid rather than a pure form" (p. 18). The first example of this genre is Karim's *al-Warda al-Bayda* (The White Rose, 1933), which stars singer and composer Muhammad Abd al-Wahhab. Finally, Fawal asserts that Kamal Salim's *al-Azima* (The Will, 1939) indexed the "maturity" of Egyptian cinema (p. 16).

The Egyptian film industry was nationalized under Gamal Abdel Nasser (1956–70) and then partially reprivatized under Anwar Sadat (1970–81). The nationalization of the film industry in 1961 was, in effect, a militarization of the film industry: "Military men, ignorant of cinema practices, were now running the studios" (Fawal, 2001, p. 42). Shafik contends that these changes did not affect the "basic commercial structure" (p. 25) of the Egyptian film industry. Furthermore, "All the popular genres created by Egyptian cinema throughout its history share the absolute determination to entertain and the permanent readiness to compromise in line with the oft-recited motto *al-gumhur 'ayiz kida* (colloquial: 'the audience wants it like this')" (Shafik, 1998/2017, p. 26, emphasis in original), which sheds light on the title of Shafik's (2006) second book, *Popular Egyptian Cinema*.

The popularity of Egyptian cinema (i.e., the aesthetic populism of its form) is a function of a basic commercial structure introduced by the early Egyptian film producers, which is practiced to this day: "the commercial exploitation" (p. 24) of anything or anyone culturally popular (e.g., songs, singers, dancers, books). This means that popular Egyptian cinema blurs the distinction between high art and low art since both are combined in a hybrid form. For example, Nobel Laureate Naguib Mahfouz worked as a screenwriter on numerous popular Egyptian films and collaborated frequently with Chahine—a vanguard figure, who also made popular films.

Murphy and Williams (2007) point out that "within film studies, Asian film has largely displaced its African counterpart as the non-Western cinema of choice" (p. 19). This is also the case with Arab cinema in general and Egyptian cinema in particular. I am not sure why Asian cinema is preferred "as the non-Western cinema of choice," but I know that African, Arab, and Egyptian cinemas are virtually unknown in Euro-America as a function of the politico-economic asymmetry between the Global North and the Global South when it comes to film distribution.

Mark Cousins's (2020) *The Story of Film* is an exceptional work of film criticism that does not neglect non-European cinema; instead, the book celebrates the accomplishments of non-European filmmakers such as Chahine, Satyajit Ray, and Moustapha al-Akkad; for example, Cousins writes about Chahine's *Bāb al-Ḥadīd* (Cairo Station, 1958) as "one of the bedrocks of the new non-aligned filmmaking" and as "a landmark of North African filmmaking" (p. 242). Cousins adds, "In the north of Africa, Egypt's master director Youssef Chahine had, for more than a decade, been challenging this mainstream [i.e., Orientalist] formula" (p. 371) of foregrounding the colonizer's gaze and voice in the context of representing Africa and Africans in (Euro-American) cinema.

"Long before German filmmakers in the 1970s did so," Cousins continues, "in films like *Cairo Station* (Egypt, 1958) he [Chahine] used the form of

American melodrama but moved to other areas of content" (p. 371), which was shocking for Egyptian spectators. As Chahine painfully recounts, "At the film's premiere, they spit in my face: 'What is this shit—who cares about a lame person?' With this film, I was told I presented a bad image of Egypt" (as cited in Salama, 2018, p. 199). Chahine adds that after the negative response to *Bāb al-Ḥadīd*, he "fell into a terrible state of depression" (p. 200), which affected him for the next five years. In *Bāb al-Ḥadīd*, Chahine plays the role of Qinawi (a crippled and sex-obsessed newspaper salesman), perhaps the first antiheroic pervert in Egyptian cinema. The charge of presenting "a bad image of Egypt" would return to haunt Chahine in response to his reflexive documentary film, *Al-Qahira Menauwwara bi Ahlaha* (Cairo Lit Up by Its People, 1991). The decolonial aesthetics of Chahine's transmodern cinema can also be described as *lit up by the undefeated spirit of the Egyptian people despite centuries of oppression.*

According to Shafik (1998/2017), "American and European imports prevailed in the film market at the time of the Arab countries' independence, together with a few Egyptian imports. (Not even in Egypt did the Egyptian share of production exceed 20 percent of all distributed films)" (p. 20). Shafik continues, "Two different strategies were developed to undermine the monopoly of Western agencies ... The first strategy consisted in monopolizing importation via public institutions, and the second in nationalizing the distribution network" (p. 21). But these strategies did not succeed beyond the Arab world, with some exceptions.

The fact that, for instance, ten of Chahine's remastered films are available on Netflix today is remarkable and promising. However, the inequities of global film distribution persist, and Chahine exhibited awareness of these inequities when he said, "The domination of Western cinema suffocates us. I only have to tell you that 280 American films are shown in the best Cairo cinemas every year! *I'm not against any culture, but ours has a right to exist too*" (as cited in Armes, 1981, p. 12, emphasis added).

Again, I would like to reiterate that Egyptian cinema is not reducible to Chahine, for while he was indeed a cinematic giant, the list of great Egyptian filmmakers includes heavyweights such as Hussein Kamal, Osama Fawzy, Salah Abu Seif, Radwan El-Kashef, Daoud Abdel Sayed, Ali Badrakhan,

Mohamed Khan, Yousry Nasrallah, Atef El-Tayeb, Fatin Abdel Wahab, Ateyyat El Abnoudy, and Khairy Beshara, as well as a newer generation of brilliant filmmakers such as Omar El Zohairy, Ayten Amin, Hala Khalil, Hala Lotfy, Kamlah Abu-Zikri, Tahani Rached, and Mohamed Diab, to name a few.

Youssef Chahine's Biography: A Decoloniality of Being

As Fawal (2001) writes, "Youssef Chahine was born in Alexandria on 25 January 1926, and apparently had a happy childhood" (p. 23). Chahine's complex subjectivity—Nasser referred to him as *al-magnoon* (the madman)—was, in effect, an embodiment of the spirit of Alexandrian cosmopolitanism he experienced growing up. His father was Lebanese, and his mother was Greek, and yet Chahine was as Egyptian as one can get, which echoes Said's (2003) point in *Freud and the Non-European* about how foundational nonidentity (or radical exteriority) is to one's identity.

According to Sigmund Freud (1939), the founder of Judaism (Moses) was non-Jewish, or Egyptian. Similarly, the most important Egyptian filmmaker (Chahine) is non-Egyptian. Cosmopolitanism is a function of the singular dash between one's identity (ego) and nonidentity (unconscious) as well as the pluriversal dash in non-European. This impossible dash at the heart of Chahine's transmodern subjectivity was often translated in his films as an irresolvable dialogue or dialectic. How one deals with this dash corresponds to the singularity of one's being vis-à-vis the radical exteriority of Other-thought. Chahine's ethico-political commitment to radical humanism was his singular/pluriversal solution to the problem of the dash. And this ethico-political commitment was embodied not only in his radical vision of cinematic worldliness but also in his daily life.

As Fawal (2001, p. 35) writes, Chahine was known to be "unpretentious" in his lifestyle, and while he was certainly famous, he invested any profits he made into making more rebellious films and paying his film crew well, which meant that the salaries for actors had to be symbolic. The meager actor salaries were not a problem because many actors wanted to work with Chahine for the experience and the prestige. For example, Mahmoud Hemeda did not mind being paid almost nothing for working with Chahine because he regarded the filmmaker as "a semi-institution" (p. 19) or a model for how to produce art films, which Hemeda replicated with his independent film production company *al-Batrik* (The Penguin). *al-Batrik* produced Osama Fawzy's surreal masterpiece *Gannat al-Shayateen* (Fallen Angels' Paradise, 1999), which launched Amr Waked's film career, for instance.

Chahine's *'insania* (humanism) may be characterized in terms of values such as *sidq* (honesty) and *shaga'a* (courage), which certainly have socialist dimensions when one considers his comradely position—a *singularity-in-comradeship*—concerning the first general strike in the history of Egyptian cinema by the Actors' Union in 1986. As Fawal recounts, "Chahine took a leading role in the whole affair. Three years later, he utilised the episode in *Alexandria Again and Forever* (1989)" (p. 50). Certainly, Chahine's *iltizam* (commitment) to representing and centering the voice of the *fellah* (peasant), particularly in his earlier films, speaks to a cinematic praxis of humanizing the oppressed and decolonizing their mind from all structures of oppression (e.g., capitalism, fundamentalism, authoritarianism, corruption). In this sense, we can read Chahine's transmodern cinema as a form of psychic decolonization: delinking from both the foreign colonizer and the native sub-oppressor.

Even though Chahine came from a modest family, his parents were determined to provide him with the best education possible, such as Victoria College in Alexandria, which was attended by the likes of Omar Sharif and Edward Said, or Pasadena Playhouse in California, where he mainly studied theater acting following Stanislavski's system. After receiving his diploma from Pasadena Playhouse in 1948, Chahine returned to Egypt to work in the publicity department of 20th Century Fox, which had an office in Cairo. Two years later, Chahine directed his first feature film *Baba Amin* (1950), at the age of twenty-four. According to Fawal (2001), "From the beginning Chahine began to lay bare parts of his autobiography, for the father in the film is modelled on his own father" (p. 38). Fawal is apt in contextualizing *Baba Amin* when he argues that the film "happened to fall in between two major historical turning points" (p. 37): *al-nakba* (catastrophe) of 1948 and the Egyptian revolution of 1952.

Chahine has directed thirty-seven feature films—out of which twelve are among the greatest one hundred Egyptian films, as selected by Egyptian film critics in 1996 through a referendum organized by the Cairo International Film Festival. Chahine is credited for introducing Omar Sharif to the silver screen with his sixth feature film *Sira' fi al-Wadi* (Struggle in the Valley, 1954). Furthermore, Fawal adds that Chahine was one of the "founders" of the Higher Cinema Institute, established in Cairo in 1959, and "a regular member of its faculty" (p. 42).

My father (Khairy), who studied there from 1963 to 1967, was taught film directing by Chahine. Chahine assigned Alexander Dean's *Fundamentals of Play Directing*, which speaks to his thespian roots; Chahine began experimenting with shadow play as a child. We can also think about Chahine's Aristotelian leftism, a thespian aesthesis undergirded by a socialist poiesis, especially vis-à-vis *Jamila* (1958), which "was his first overtly political film to date" (p. 41).

Chahine's genius as a cineaste was recognized internationally, particularly in the 1990s, through retrospectives, special issues, and lifetime achievement awards by the Locarno Film Festival (1996), *Cahiers du cinéma* (1996), the Cannes Film Festival (1997), and the Lincoln Film Center (1998). Chahine continues to be posthumously remembered and celebrated with film screenings in Egypt, Saudi Arabia, France, Germany, and Switzerland, among other places, and yet he remains virtually unknown—a paradox that necessitates this dual sociology of absences and emergences.

Fawal asserts that Chahine's filmography can be grouped into three periods: (1) the early period (1952–70), (2) the middle period (1970–81), and (3) the late period (1981–2007). Each period is associated with the reign of a specific president: Nasser, Sadat, and Mubarak, respectively. However, it is more historically accurate to think of the first period as between the Egyptian revolution of 1952 and *al-naksa* of 1968, for it captures the postcolonial ideology of Arab nationalism: Arab socialism.

The second period corresponds to Sadat's *infitah*, or open-door policy, which reversed Nasser's socialist legacy of nationalization and agrarian reforms through privatization and foreign capital investment. While Egypt did not technically win the Yom Kippur War, Sadat won a decisive battle on

October 6, 1973, against the Israeli occupiers in the Sinai Peninsula. Sadat was willing to do anything to retrieve Sinai, which was returned to Egypt after the signing of the Camp David Accords in 1978. The peace treaty is still considered controversial among many Arabs today, for it signifies normalization with Israel, which is perceived as a settler-colonial state. Muslim fundamentalists assassinated Sadat three years later due to his contentious but daring decision.

Chahine did not live long enough to experience the Egyptian uprising of 2011, but his films have contributed to a collective sedimentation of a revolutionary consciousness, critical of oppressive ideologies (cf. Ismat, 2019). Even Chahine's last—and most commercially successful—film *Heya Fawda?* (Is This Chaos?, 2007) exposes the corruption of the Egyptian police under Mubarak, which was one of the main reasons for protestors organizing the 2011 uprising on National Police Day, or January 25. The mass-mediated videos and images of the brutal killing of Alexandrian activist Khaled Saeed by police officers in 2010 were the straw that broke the camel's back. Therefore, Chahine's late period corresponds to the corrupt regime of Hosni Mubarak, and his late style can be read as a critique of postmodern/postcolonial acquiescence in Mubarak's Egypt, which manifested materially in terms of an intensifying dialectical relationship between parasitic capitalism and Islamic fundamentalism, as Wahba (1995/2022) shows. In sum, Chahine's prolific filmography provides his spectators with poetic and aesthetic answers to Galal Amin's (2000) question: "Whatever happened to the Egyptians?"

In addition to periodizing Chahine's filmography, Fawal groups his films into four distinct genres: (1) social dramas and melodramas, (2) wartime and postwar films, (3) autobiographical "trilogy," and (4) historical films. Under social dramas and melodramas, Fawal includes *Bab al-Hadid* (Cairo Station, 1958) and *al-Ard* (The Land, 1969). Wartime and postwar films consist of *Jamila al-Jaza'iriyaa* (Jamila the Algerian, 1958), *al-Asfour* (The Sparrow, 1972), and *Awdat al-Ibn al-Dal* (Return of the Prodigal Son, 1976). The autobiographical "trilogy" is now a quartet with the installment of *Alexandria ... New York* (2004), released three years after the publication of Fawal's book. Under historical films, Fawal lists *al-Nasir Salah al-Din* (Saladin, 1963), *Adieu*

Bonaparte (1985), *al-Mohager* (The Emigrant, 1994), and *al-Maṣīr* (The Destiny, 1997). Nevertheless, Fawal holds:

> Chahine has developed his own film-making style, which is characteristically frenetic, non-linear, multi-layered, cerebral and demanding. Many of his films "read" like modernist scripts: fragmented, convoluted, with a dash of the Theatre of the Absurd. Of particular interest to his admirers is his innovative use of time, space, *mise-en-scène*, memory, and the blending of genres in a single film. (pp. 1–2, emphasis in original)

In sum, Chahine's "complex cinema of ideas" (p. 1) is a function of his transmodern subjectivity. As a border filmmaker, Chahine was able, through an ethico-political commitment to radical humanism, to translate the singularity of his being into a pluriversal aesthetic that was cosmopolitan in form yet Egyptian in content—this is what I mean by *cinematic worldliness* or *transmodern cinema*.

Chahine's awareness of his double-consciousness came about when he was a student in the United States after he realized that he was not given a chance to play Hamlet—his favorite dramatic character since adolescence—because he was a "little African with a big nose and big ears" (as cited in Fawal, 2001, p. 32). Even though Chahine graduated as a top student from Pasadena Playhouse, which was no easy feat, his awareness of how he was perceived by the Gaze of the Euro-American Other led him to abandon acting for directing.

Of course, Chahine would never completely abandon acting but return to it on his own terms, as attested by his masterful performances in *Cairo Station* (1958) and *Alexandria: Again and Forever* (1989). It is interesting to note Chahine's identification with the character of Hamlet in several of his films, given Simon Critchley and Jamieson Webster's (2013) remark that William Shakespeare's (1602) *Hamlet* is "a play about nothing." For Chahine, this nothingness, or nonbeing, was specifically the Other of the Other, which, as he recounts, was negated by the Euro-American Other. As such, Chahine's ethico-political filmography exemplifies the negation of the negation through his poetic/aesthetic affirmation of the non-European Other or his self-representation of radical exteriority. Therefore, Chahine's cinematic worldliness affirms the historical reason of the Other in both totality and exteriority.

4

The Decoloniality of Poetics: *al-Maṣīr* (1997)

al-Maṣīr—Chahine's most successful film in France—is a history of the present and an allegorical autobiography. To provide some context, the film was released in 1997. On November 17th of that year, a terrorist attack known as the "Luxor massacre" occurred, wherein a group of six Muslim fundamentalists associated with al-Gama'a al-Islamiyya (the Islamic Group), but disguised as security officers, killed sixty-two civilians in the courtyard of Temple of Hatshepsut. The majority of these civilians were tourists. This bloody event underlines the political urgency of *al-Maṣīr* as a film about the historical yet ongoing struggle between fundamentalism and secularization, which can be qualified as a class struggle given that workers stand to lose the most in the unfolding dialectic between parasitic capitalism and religious fundamentalism.

al-Maṣīr was a political response to two specific events that took place in 1994: the stabbing of his close friend (novelist Naguib Mahfouz) and the banning of Chahine's previous film *al-Mohager*. More subtly, the film is also a critique of actor Mohsen Mohieddin, who began his film career portraying Chahine in *Iskandaria … leh?* (1979), but then decided to quit acting in the early 1990s for religious reasons.

Therefore, in *al-Maṣīr*, Ibn Rushd (the philosopher) represents Chahine, Marwan (the poet) represents Mahfouz, and Abdallah (the dancer turned fundamentalist; see Figure 9) represents Mohieddin—not to mention that twelfth-century Córdoba represents Chahine's Alexandria. And so we see the banning of Ibn Rushd's books, repeating the banning of *al-Mohager*. We also observe Marwan (played by Mohamed Mounir) being stabbed in the neck by fundamentalists the same way Mahfouz was stabbed. And finally, we witness how fundamentalists lure Abdallah (played by Hani Salama), the

Figures 9 and 10 Abdallah between secularization and fundamentalism.

Source: Misr International Films.

Caliph's younger son, through flattery away from the joys of life—dancing for Abdallah, or acting for Mohieddin. The fundamentalists in the film are members of a death-driven cult (see Figure 10) whose symptoms include mortification of the flesh and blind allegiance to a "pure" leader (emir). While fascism is certainly a twentieth-century phenomenon, Chahine's history of the present presents us with a genealogy of fascism, whose elements include authoritarianism, nationalism, and militarism.

The fundamentalist cult is referred to in the film as al-Gama'a (the Group), which is one of the references for the Muslim Brotherhood—a transnational Islamic fundamentalist organization that was founded in 1928 by Hassan al-Banna with its headquarters being located in Egypt. The abovementioned terrorist group (al-Gama'a al-Islamiyya) responsible for the Luxor massacre is an offshoot of the Muslim Brotherhood, and it prefers violent militancy to electoral politics—the latter being the preferred political strategy of the Muslim Brotherhood.

In *al-Maṣīr*, the fundamentalist cult is portrayed as a paramilitary group organized hierarchically through blind allegiance to the emir. The emir is a puppet controlled by Sheikh Riad (played by Ahmed Fouad Selim)—an influential theologian in the court of Caliph al-Mansur (played by Mahmoud Hemida). Sheikh Riad pulls the strings from behind the scenes and plays even with the Caliph as a pawn on his chessboard, which is how the Caliph eventually turns against Ibn Rushd (played by Nour el-Sherif). Sheikh Riad even allies himself with the Caliph's enemies, such as the Spaniards, and attempts unsuccessfully to turn his older son, Crown Prince al-Nasir (played by Khaled Nabawy; see Figure 11), against his father.

In a pivotal scene, the Caliph is arguing with his brother about the relevance of Ibn Rushd and his philosophy, which he finds threatening to his authority since it affirms *the authority of reason* over *the authoritarianism of the ruler*. The Caliph's brother says, "Ideas have wings. No one can prevent them from reaching people." The Caliph replies in anger, "I can! I am al-Andalus." We hear his statement echoed, for they are standing in the palace courtyard, and we see them in a wide overhead shot. Chahine shows that an authoritarian ruler, blinded by vanity, can be easily exploited by fundamentalist theologians, for authoritarianism implies a lack of power and legitimacy, hence insecurity

Figure 11 Crown Prince al-Nasir.
Source: Misr International Films.

in both senses of the word: psychological and political. On the other hand, Ibn Rushd's commitment to the authority of reason entails respect for truth and justice, wherein no one is above the law—not even the Caliph.

The specific incident that alienated the Caliph from Ibn Rushd concerns the trial of Marwan's stabber. The Caliph wanted the convict to be executed without trial; however, Ibn Rushd tried the convict and decided to send him to prison instead of executing him as the Caliph wished. The conflict between the Caliph and Ibn Rushd on this ruling leads the latter to resign from his post as chief judge of Córdoba. In the background, the fundamentalists successfully recruit the Caliph's younger son Abdallah and train him to kill his father, burn Ibn Rushd's library, and eventually kill Marwan—an event that opens Abdallah's eyes to the truth of fundamentalism: terrorism. Ibn Rushd, however, manages—with help from his students and friends—to make copies of his books, store them in his cellar (see Figure 12), and send copies elsewhere for safekeeping. One of those destinations is Egypt, a commentary

Figure 12 Ibn Rushd and Abdallah in the cellar after the book burning.
Source: Misr International Films.

on the country's enlightened role as a beacon of Islamic humanism at one point in time.

The film ends on a cautionary note: the burning of Ibn Rushd's books and his exile along with his family from Córdoba. The shot of the flames (see Figure 13) is a bookend, for it repeats an early shot in the film: the burning of Joseph's father at the stake by the Church authorities in Languedoc, France. His crime was translating the works of heretic philosopher Ibn Rushd from Arabic to Latin. Images and videos of book burning in the twentieth century are typically associated with Nazi book burnings, which again stresses my point about the film as a history of the present and as a genealogy of fascism with its roots in authoritarianism and fundamentalism.

Mourad Wahba (1995/2022) defines fundamentalism as *thinking of what is relative in absolute terms*, wherein *absolutism signifies nonthinking or lack of critical thinking*. In the film, we see the fundamentalists using rhetorical reasoning, such as flattery—and other forms of persuasion—as a political recruitment tool. To say that Chahine's transmodern cinema is secular means

Figure 13 Ibn Rushd during the public burning of his books.
Source: Misr International Films.

that it is a cinema that values postabyssal thinking, historical reasoning, and secular critique, a cinema that celebrates life, love, music, dance, beauty, humanity, and so on. In other words, Chahine's cinema celebrates the radical possibility of cinema everywhere. Fundamentalism means the impossibility of cinema, which is equivalent to death for Chahine.

In sum, *al-Maṣīr* deals with the questions of authority and secularization through their crisis versions: authoritarianism and fundamentalism. The film posits this crisis as an outcome of the social struggle between death-driven instrumental reason and life-driven historical reason. When it comes to ethics, politics, and aesthetics, the people (and the spectators), like the Caliph, must choose between the sophistry of authoritarians and the poetics of philosophers: the falsehood of instrumental reason and fundamentalism versus the truth of historical reason and secularization.

For Chahine (the author), authority stems from poetic reason. Similarly, power arises from democratic legitimacy. Adeeb (poet) is Chahine's middle name, and it means a man of letters who is also of virtuous character. In the next section, I will apply the "savage" methodology of decolonial film theory to a close analysis of *al-Maṣīr* (cf. Vàzquez, 2020). Decolonial film theory is "savage" because it is radically exterior to, and a critique of, (colonial) film theory. The latter assumes its totalizing theory to be "civilized" or sophisticated when its (mis)representation of the non-European Other is either Orientalist or nonexistent. A central part of any decolonial method is contextualizing and historizing non-European subjects and objects to give voice to that which has been ideologically silenced or erased in Eurocentric modern/colonial discourses and fantasies. As Michel-Rolph Trouillot (1995) asserts:

> Silences enter the process of historical production at four crucial moments: the moment of fact creation (the making of *sources*); the moment of fact assembly (the making of *archives*); the moment of fact retrieval (the making of *narratives*); and the moment of retrospective significance (the making of *history* in the final instance). (p. 26, emphasis in original)

To undo the violence of silencing, Chahine uses "*joie de vivre* [see Figure 14], music, dance—and, of course, reason" (as cited in Fargeon, 1997,

Figure 14 Ibn Rushd's *joie de vivre*.
Source: Misr International Films.

p. 48, emphasis in original). Therefore, any decolonial method must follow historical reason, wherein the question of *aesthetic, ethical, and political enjoyment* is framed in the context of world modernity and liberation praxis. The decolonial film theorist is a cinephile who enjoys masterpieces from around the world and is committed to critiquing films and film theory from the position of radical exteriority, which entails border thinking, delinking, intercultural translation, ecologies of knowledges, and so on.

The "Savage" Methodology of Decolonial Film Theory

1. Modernity of Space

In (colonial) cinema, non-European spaces are often represented in an Orientalist fashion, as exotic or "barbarian," which occludes their alter-modernity behind non-European mystique. Arab modernity, for instance, is an anticolonial project grounded in Arab poetics; as I have argued earlier, Arab modernity precedes Euromodernity, which began with the colonization of the Americas in the fifteenth century and expanded through the world systematization of racial capitalism as an apparatus of domination.

When it comes to cinematic representations of the Orient, particularly the Arab world, we are often bombarded with negative stereotypes that associate Arabness with despotism, backwardness, terrorism, or premodernity in general; in other words, the "barbarian" space is a hostile space, which justifies not going there cinematically or representing this space as desirable only in terms of resources (e.g., oil) but not otherwise. In his magnum opus, Said (1978/2003) writes about the conceptual importance of space and geography when analyzing Orientalist representations. He argues that Orientalism is

> a *distribution* of geopolitical awareness into aesthetic, scholarly, economic, sociological, historical, and philological texts; it is an *elaboration* not only of a basic geographical distinction (the world is made up of two unequal halves, Orient and Occident) but also of a whole series of "interests" which, by such means as scholarly discovery, philological reconstruction, psychological

The Decoloniality of Poetics: al-Maṣīr *(1997)* 139

analysis, landscape and sociological description, it not only creates but also maintains. (p. 12, emphasis in original)

Therefore, (colonial) cinema is inherently Orientalist primarily as a function of what Said calls "imaginative geography" (p. 54), which is an arbitrary geographical distinction between two spaces: civilization and barbarism, or the West and the rest. al-Andalus with its borderland spatiality complicates this geographical distinction as an Islamic polity inside Europe—a radical exteriority within Europe's spatial imagination, a case of traumatic nonidentity. Imaginative geography in (colonial) cinema dramatizes "the distance and difference between what is close and what is far away" (p. 55); decolonial cinema, on the other hand, explodes this dramatization.

In *al-Maṣīr*, Chahine disrupts the imaginative geography of (colonial) cinema by representing al-Andalus in a non-Orientalist way, as a borderland space, which allows the spectator to appreciate the poetics of Arab modernity and the aesthetics of Islamic humanism as embodied in terms of architecture, design, philosophy, poetry, music, and so on. As I have mentioned before, the nonfigurative aesthetics of Islamic art anticipated the abstract impulse of modern European art by centuries (Shabout, 2007). Furthermore, as Malek Khouri (2010) writes about *al-Maṣīr*'s mise-en-scène:

The film's representation of life in Andalusia selects landscapes, costumes, architectural exteriors, and interiors that, as signifiers, destabilize dominant western imaging (as well as fundamentalist ahistoric nostalgia for a misconstrued past) of an Arab Orient characterized by dusty deserts, clay architecture, and women covered in black from head to toe. (p. 180)

The pluriversal politics in the Caliphate of Córdoba presents the spectator with an essential lesson about cultural heterogeneity for the Arab internationalist project to come. For example, as Khouri (2010) points out, in the film, we enjoy "the coalescence of Spanish, Arab, and Gypsy dance traditions" (p. 179) that reflects the cultural pluralism of al-Andalus as a borderland spatiality. As such, *al-Maṣīr* embodies a heterogeneity of styles and cannot be classified into one genre, for the film shifts stylistically between the historical, the musical, and the melodramatic—and sometimes even the comedic. Barbara Lekatsas (2014) asserts that Chahine's "style of mixing genres—the musical, newsreels, love story, etc.—and the stark juxtaposition of the personal with the political creates a surreal effect, a layered palimpsest" (p. 141).

In Khouri's (2010) words, *al-Maṣīr* "breaks down the artificial barriers—of form, geography, high and low art, performer and artist—that so often demarcate cinematic cultural practices in the west," which "allows the film to effectively reach out to a wide audience with an urgent message of relevance to regional and world politics" (p. 178). Josef Gugler (2011) makes a similar argument when he writes, "If Chahine draws on the traditions of Egyptian cinema [e.g., melodrama and musical] and Hollywood [e.g., romance and suspense] to provide thrilling entertainment, he also transcends them" (p. 254). Gugler adds, "The song and dance sequences, seamlessly integrated into the action, serve to complement the philosopher's teachings with Chahine's philosophy of *joie de vivre*" (pp. 254–5, emphasis in original). In other words, Chahine shows that, *for transmodern subjectivity, aesthetic enjoyment sustains poetic reason.* Dave Kehr (1996) recognizes this enjoyable dimension on a felt level when he writes:

> Chahine refuses to invest anything less than his full talent on the level of shot and sequence. Consequently, even the least of his films gives off a sense of *physical pleasure* and *sensual engagement*, like eating a wonderful meal or touching a fine piece of fabric. (p. 25, emphasis added)

2. Coloniality of Time

In colonial cinema, the non-European world is represented as before time or outside history—that is, as "primitive." Alejandro Vallega (2014a) writes about this phenomenon as the "coloniality of time," which Said (1978/2003) addresses in terms of "historical knowledge." Said writes, "Psychologically, Orientalism is a form of paranoia, knowledge of another kind, say, from ordinary historical knowledge" (p. 72). I have been addressing this question of time throughout the book in terms of historical reason, which signifies *the liberatory teleology of world modernity* as opposed to the violent and oppressive reality of ethnocentric modernization/colonization. *al-Maṣīr* raises the question of how the Arabs can be considered "primitive" when the Islamic Golden Age preceded the European Renaissance.

To explore this question, Chahine resorts to a nonlinear narrative structure, or anachronic temporality. While the plot is linear, the narrative is nonlinear as a history of the present, for it is an allegorical autobiography. As Ibrahim al-Ariss (2009) writes, "Rarely was an Arab film capable of swinging between the past and the present the way *al-Maṣīr* did" (p. 212). If anything, the arrow of time for Chahine moves in the direction of the past and not the future, which deconstructs the modern myth of progress—a rhetoric whose logic erases the colonial history of genocide, enslavement, and exploitation. The progress of world modernity, therefore, is *nonlinear*. It exists *when* historical reason is put in the service of collective liberation.

In the words of Khouri (2010), "Chahine forges an inter-textuality linking the past, the present, and the possibilities for future change: a sort of cultural memory" (p. 183). *al-Maṣīr* is not a nostalgic fantasy about the past; instead, it is a representation of a collective memory (the Islamic Golden Age), which is indexed primarily as a reminder of *the liberation ethics of Islamic humanism*—an ethics of difference grounded in textual interpretation. As such, Chahine is suggesting, with his politicization of aesthetics, that *cinema itself has the potential to be decolonial when it affirms the authority of poetic reason*. Decolonial cinema is a transmodern praxis of liberation, which rejects all forms of authoritarianism: racial capitalism, colonialism, imperialism, militarism, fundamentalism, and so on.

Chahine asserts, "Without memory, we are doomed to repeat the mistakes of the past ... All golden ages have emerged from periods of tolerance" (as cited in Fargeon, 1997, p. 47). His Freudian statement sheds light on the logic of authoritarian enjoyment: the symptomatic repetition of violence. Violence is repeated symptomatically when the bearers of the Absolute Truth, who are also literalists, reject textual interpretation and intercultural translation as methodologies that produce ecologies of knowledges. The humanistic (and psychoanalytic) intervention involves working dialogically through our political differences, thereby eschewing the unconscious repetition of violence. Authoritarian violence can be either symbolic or physical. Chahine suggests that symbolic violence is worse, "the worst kind of violence is perhaps to say to someone: 'Everything you write will be burned' " (p. 48).

The characters in *al-Maṣīr* speak in a contemporary Egyptian dialect as opposed to classical Arabic (or *Fuṣḥa*), which is typically used in historical epics. By ignoring this convention, Chahine is consciously condensing the time between the past and the present: a condensation of eight centuries. He condenses time to historicize the present, which is a political act. Khouri (2010) writes, "The colloquial spoken word reflects Chahine's interest in an oral text accessible to his audience, while on the ideological level it also represents a break from the dogmatic presentation of history through the mediation of high and sanctified text" (p. 182).

In other words, the use of colloquial speech secularizes the sacredness of Arabic (the language of the Qur'ān), thereby opening the cinematic text to allegorical interpretation, which affords the film to be a pluriversal political commentary on the failure of the Arab national project. Chahine then associates Arab modernity with the poetic function of the Arabic language "as a dynamic signifier of history" (p. 182).

Throughout the film, Marwan sings as a form of resistance to fundamentalism; fundamentalism terrorizes the Other to silence difference. The film's central theme is captured in Marwan's key song, which he repeats on multiple occasions: "Raise your voice through singing, for songs are still possible." It is interesting to think about Chahine's cinematic praxis of centering the *ughniya* in light of the following words from Irish singer and songwriter Glen Hansard, "Those who are the victors write the history. And those who suffered wrote the songs." Fundamentalists silence the Other through various forms of intimidation, ranging from symbolic violence (e.g., book burning or exile) to physical violence (e.g., stabbing or killing). Marwan was finally silenced when the fundamentalists murdered him. However, for Chahine, fundamentalism will never prevail because, as he puts it in the film's closing statement, which is superimposed on a closeup shot of flames burning Ibn Rushd's books: "Ideas have wings. No one can prevent them from reaching people." Stretching Chahine's premise, I would add that *Other-thought and transmodern cinema have wings, too.* The negation of non-European cinema speaks to the fundamentalism of Euro-American cinema and film theory. Its silence, in effect, is a form of censorship.

Figure 15 Marwan.
Source: Misr International Films.

3. Colonial Difference: From Film Theory to Decolonial Film Theory

Colonial difference is the difference between *the instrumental reason of modernity/coloniality* and *the historical reason of transmodernity/ decoloniality*; the latter is the worlding of liberatory modernity through radical exteriority. For our purposes, colonial difference is the distinction between (colonial) cinema and decolonial cinema as well as between (colonial) film theory and decolonial film theory. As such, I have described the latter as a "savage" methodology because the decolonial film theorist, typically a "savage" of the non-European variety, aims to decolonize the "civilized" aesthetics of Euro-American cinema and deconstruct the coloniality of Euro-American film theory.

I will focus on six authoritative texts of film theory to demonstrate the coloniality of Euro-American film theory, or how its modern/colonial politics of citation enacts a negation of non-European cinema. If we combine the six books and treat them as a single source, then film scholars have cited them around 10,382 times. In *The Major Film Theories*, J. Dudley Andrew (1976) has nothing to say about non-European cinema. In a later book, *Concepts in Film Theory*, Andrew (1984) has only a passing reference to "recent interest in the study of Third World films" (p. 161), which is to say that he acknowledges that other unnamed film scholars are interested in non-European cinema, but not him. Similarly, in *Film Theory: An Introduction*, Robert Lapsley and Michael Westlake (1988) make no mention whatsoever of non-European cinema, and when they address the non-European, this is what they write: "The element 'Indian' in the opposition European/Indian may be aligned with the element 'savage' in one film and with the element 'civilised' in another" (p. 110). *Film Theory and Criticism* is an anthology book coedited by Gerald Mast, Marshall Cohen, and Leo Braudy (1992) and, as of the fourth edition, there are zero contributions from non-European theorists or filmmakers. Similarly, there are no references at all to non-European cinema in Siegfried Kracauer's (1997) *Theory of Film*.

However, Robert Stam's (2000) *Film Theory: An Introduction* is somewhat of a wonderful exception, for he actually includes a section in the book on "Third World Film and Theory," wherein he cites Chahine to demonstrate his point about the "cross-fertilization between Italian neo-realism and film theory and practice" (p. 93) in the Global South. While I respect Stam's effort at including non-European cinema, I worry about the assimilationist trap of including the Other into the same, wherein exteriority is tamed by the totality of the modern system.

(Colonial) film theory tames non-European cinema by underemphasizing its originality while highlighting its derivative quality. Non-European cinema then becomes relatable only in terms of mimicry, or how much it is influenced by European cinema. Nevertheless, Stam is a sincere comrade, particularly when he acknowledges, "There have been many modernist and avant-garde films in the Third World" (p. 156) since the 1920s, or when he mindfully explores ethical questions in sections such as "Multiculturalism, Race, and Representation" and "Third Cinema Revisited." Not mentioning his other radical publications, such as his coauthorship with Ella Shohat of *Unthinking Eurocentrism* (1994), or his more recent *Indigeneity and the Decolonizing Gaze*

(2022). As such, Stam stands out in the colonial field of film theory because he exhibits true solidarity with the oppressed by considering non-European cinema on its own terms. This critical trend, which he represents, is clearly a minor current; nevertheless, Stam's delinking from the coloniality of film theory—a coloniality of power/knowledge/being—is a commendable effort.

Furthermore, Stam (2000) deserves credit for acknowledging the alter-modernity of non-European cinema, particularly when he writes, "What we now call Third World cinema, taken in a broad sense, far from being a marginal appendage to First World cinema, has actually produced *most* of the world's feature films" (p. 21, emphasis in original). Consequently, non-European cinema ought to be considered *major cinema*—my notion of *transmodern cinema* is an attempt in that direction.

Perhaps non-European cinema names a Hegelian third term beyond the deadlock of (colonial) film theory, which is still plagued by a racial capitalist hierarchical ideology: First World cinema as the nobility, Second World cinema as the clergy, and Third World cinema as the commoners (p. 93). As such, I agree with Stam's definition of Third Cinema as "a revolutionary cinema" without reducing it exclusively to "militant guerrilla documentaries" (p. 96). Mignolo and Walsh (2018) conceive of decoloniality, among other things, as an "option." Therefore, decolonial cinema presents us with an aesthetic third option beyond the cinematic coloniality of the nobility and the cinematic postcoloniality of the clergy. The cinematic decoloniality of the commoners then is a critique of racial capitalism, particularly the authoritarianism of this oppressive/violent apparatus in the form of either militarism or fundamentalism.

The history of film theory is indeed a world history of racialized class struggles. While I admire Stam's reflexivity in his careful treatment of non-European cinema, I do not find the designation of Third World cinema to be "empowering" (p. 100), as he claims, for he even compares it to "cinema" as opposed to First World cinema, in particular. The signifier "cinema" does not need to be qualified, according to him, for it unconsciously means First World cinema.

I also appreciate Stam's section on "Film and the Postcolonial," but my emphasis on decolonial cinema is a critique of both colonial and postcolonial cinemas. I am interested in anticolonial non-European cinema as opposed to non-European films produced after the formal end of colonial rule. Neocolonialism and endocolonization continue to persist in the (post)colonial world, hence the need for self-criticism vis-à-vis sub-oppression—that is, the colonized intellectual's internalization of colonial oppression.

What I find empowering is writing an entire book, as opposed to a few sections, on a specific Egyptian filmmaker (Chahine) while referencing mostly non-European scholars to make a radical argument about the cinematic worldliness of non-European cinema. That is more emancipating, in my view, than referencing Third World cinema in a generic way as an insignificant movement outside of Euromodernity.

The Other-thought of decolonial film theory is enacted using decolonial concepts and methods (e.g., delinking, border thinking, intercultural translation) in an effort to prefigure an ethico-political transmodern world to come through the aesthetics and poetics of transmodern cinema. I have been practicing this decolonizing/deconstructing from the perspective of radical exteriority by emphasizing the historical reason of Arab modernity and Islamic humanism, which translate in terms of transmodern poetics and decolonial aesthetics in the philosophy of Ibn Rushd and the cinema of Youssef Chahine, respectively.

We cannot see Chahine's transmodern cinema through the lens of (colonial) film theory, for it either does not exist or exists as auteur cinema, world cinema, or any other conceptual category preferred by the masters of film theory. My effort throughout the book has been to theorize and historicize Chahine's cinema on its own terms, particularly as exemplary of *cinematic worldliness* given its decolonial emphasis on radical humanism, pluriversal politics, ethics of liberation, ecologies of knowledges, and so on. Furthermore, self-criticism (cf. al-Azm, 2011) is a central feature of decolonial film theory because to arrive at the *best* of modernity and its alterity in cinema or otherwise, we must be able to criticize the unethical dimensions of not only modernity but also alterity, which is why I have critiqued the violence of both colonial oppression and (post)colonial sub-oppression. Decolonial film theory champions any transmodern cinematic self-representation, which foregrounds a decoloniality of power/knowledge/being.

4. The Transmodernity/Decoloniality of Cinematic Worldliness

My argument regarding cinematic worldliness is that Chahine's radical humanism is more universal than the antihumanism of Hollywood cinema— the latter being ideological cinema par excellence. Chahine's transmodern cinema stretches the modern rhetoric of cinema beyond its colonial logic, which seeks to exterminate aesthetic/poetic differences through assimilation or extinction. The "third-world" filmmaker is expected to assimilate into the Hollywood system or die on the hill of "world cinema"—a niche hill, to say the least.

Hollywood cinema is ideological in two senses: (1) in its fundamentalist absolutization of the racial capitalist world-system (thus dehumanizing racialized workers) and (2) in its mythologization of nostalgic fantasies that tame the trauma of desire (thus dehumanizing political subjectivity in both totality and exteriority). Conversely, Chahine's transmodern cinema embodies a material critique of ideology in at least two ways: (1) rejecting the authoritarianism of oppressive modernization/colonization (while affirming the historical reason of Arab modernity) and (2) rejecting fundamentalism (while affirming the secularizing potential of Islamic humanism). Without steps 1 and 2, transmodernity and decoloniality would not be possible.

The rejection of fundamentalism is clear in *al-Maṣīr*, and it is accomplished cinematically through a Manichean aesthetic, which juxtaposes the dark world of the fundamentalists with the enlightened world of the philosophers and the poets. For example, whereas the fundamentalists are dressed in duo-chromatic uniforms (green and white), the wardrobe on the other side is multicolored and vibrant, reflecting cultural diversity. Also, the fundamentalists engage in an ominous style of mystical chanting (i.e., *dhikr*) accompanied by nauseating and repetitive body movements, which leads some cult members to collapse. This imagery of fervent worship is reminiscent of the Pentecostal practice labeled Slain in the Spirit, wherein the Holy Spirit renders Christian believers unconscious.

The rejection of modernization/colonization is less evident in the film, but it is present in Chahine's affirmation of Arab modernity in the twelfth century as constitutive of the pluriversal politics of al-Andalus, which was later displaced by Euro-Christian modernity/coloniality beginning with the *Reconquista*. Chahine rejects oppressive modernization/colonization through his critique of the Caliph's authoritarianism—which, according to the film's anachronic temporality, would also be a critique of Mubarak. To counter the two reactionary tendencies, which he rejects, Chahine foregrounds secularization and the authority of reason as correctives.

Furthermore, Chahine frames the Caliphate as a pluriversal political system that has an internationalist potential. However, he also shows how internationalism regresses into nationalism through the instrumental marriage between fundamentalism and authoritarianism, thus aborting the democratic spirit of secularization, which is based on the authority of reason. In sum, Chahine's transmodern cinema prefigures Arab internationalism as a secular democratic project of liberation, which is inherently modern and humanist, and yet not Eurocentric—because world modernity and radical humanism are attributes of civilization, which are not exclusive to any specific culture.

Figure 16 Caliph al-Mansur.
Source: Misr International Films.

Chahine's Decolonial Cinema and Its Transmodern Poetics of Liberation

al-Maṣīr is a poetic retelling, in film form, of the life of Ibn Rushd; in other words, Chahine's focus is on the elements of film form as opposed to historical accuracy. According to Aristotle, "It is not the poet's function to relate actual events, but the *kinds* of things that might occur and are possible in terms of probability or necessity" (1995, p. 59, emphasis in original). Aristotle's distinction between the poet and historian sheds light on Chahine's poetic reasoning, or why he thought it was essential to produce and release *al-Maṣīr* in 1997 to an Arabic-speaking audience in Egypt and the rest of the Arab world.

Chahine made *al-Maṣīr* not because of what happened to Ibn Rushd or Chahine himself, as we shall see, but because of *what might happen to poets like Ibn Rushd or Chahine in the future*. In this sense, the film is a cautionary tale. By characterizing both Ibn Rushd and Chahine as poets, I am following Ibn Rushd's argument that "poetical discourse is a form of logical discourse" (Fakhry, 2001, p. 41), which is "liable to truth or falsity" (p. 42).

The stakes of the film's poetic function are raised when one considers Mona Abousenna's argument that Chahine—along with Taha Hussein and Naguib Mahfouz—is a modern example of Ibn Rushd (as cited in Wahba & Abousenna, 1996, p. 108)—that is, a heretic. Abousenna draws a parallel between "the climate of takfir, or charge of blasphemy" (p. 107) against Ibn Rushd in the twelfth century and Chahine in the twentieth century. The latter created a stir with his 1994 film *al-Mohager* (The Emigrant), about the prophet Joseph, which happens to be Chahine's first name.

Actor Khaled el Nabawy portrayed Joseph despite the Islamic prohibition on figural representations of Allāh and His prophets. Therefore, we can read *al-Maṣīr* as Chahine's delayed response—after three years—to the controversy surrounding his previous film, *al-Mohager*. And we can also assert, following Abousenna, that Chahine identified with Ibn Rushd; in other words, *al-Maṣīr* is not only a historical drama but also an autobiographical tragedy (cf. al-Ariss, 2009), wherein Chahine is exposing us to a mode of poetic enjoyment that he finds lacking (or impossible) in his contemporary sociopolitical reality, which for him mirrors the end of the Islamic Golden Age and the failure of *al-nahḍa*. The film then raises the question: can we (the spectators) align our desires with Ibn Rushd's (and Chahine's) desire for truth, justice, and beauty?

Ibn Rushd's (and Chahine's) desire is more accurately a desire, which is actualized in methods of interpretation or forms of reasoning as poetic processes of historical knowledge production. In other words, desiring is more about the journey than the destination, which may sound ironic given the film's title: *al-Maṣīr* (The Destiny), but the journey is the destination. In Islam, everything is predestined (*al-qaḍā' wa-l-qadr*) or written (*maktub*). However, only Allāh knows what is written. Therefore, it is erroneous for the fundamentalists to assume that they have access to this knowledge, which Wahba (1995/2022) qualifies as "the Absolute Truth." To put it differently, historical reason is the poetic path of desiring knowledge *qua* relative truth; the dogmatic negation of historical reason is the end of desire and truth, that is, of life and meaning.

There are at least two types of destiny: (1) psychic destiny, which is Ibn Rushd's unity of intellect doctrine: the conjunction (*ittiṣāl*) of the material intellect with the active intellect (cf. Fakhry, 2004, p. 301); and (2) social destiny, which is the ideal form of the *ummah* as "the [single] universal community of piety and justice" (Ansary, 2009, p. 118). Social destiny is theoretically there in the Qur'ān; in practice, the *ummah* has been, for the most part, a pluriversal polity, such as the period when the three caliphates of the Umayyads, Abbāsids, and Fāṭimids overlapped.

Psychic destiny, on the other hand, is a concept that Ibn Rushd borrows from one of his teachers (Ibn Bājja), who was himself inspired by Ibn Sīnā's Neoplatonist reading of Aristotelian contemplation. Conjunction with the active intellect amounts to "the attainment of a spiritual or intellectual condition in which the mind is united with this supermundane agency and thereby becomes a part of the intelligible world" (p. 217). Robert Solomon and Kathleen Higgins (1996) clarify, "Ibn Rushd accepted the traditional Islamic doctrine of the immortality of the soul" (p. 138). However, what survives death is not the soul per se but the material intellect as a potentiality actualized in the active intellect—the transcendent and universal form of the intellect (cf.

Fakhry, 2001, pp. 70–3). The unity of the intellect is the liberationist telos of historical reason.

James Hollis (2009) writes, "Fate is what is given to us; destiny is what we are summoned to become" (p. 324). In other words, along the lines of *amor fati*, destiny—or the journey of destination—is how we subjectify our fate, that is, making what is given to us our own. The heretic (e.g., Ibn Rushd or Chahine) chooses historical reason, or the examined life, as poetic means to fatalistic ends despite the dangers posed by the dogmatists, from exile to death. Ibn Rushd's books were burned, and such a symbolic negation of reason is certainly one of the formal elements of fascism, as in the spectacle of the 1933 Nazi book burnings.

The dogmatic negation of reason through burning, banning, or killing is premised on a politics of sameness; on the other hand, historical reason opens up the traumatic dimension of difference—or of "political dissensus" according to Rancière (2014). A fundamentalist politics of sameness is at the root of any authoritarian political project. Conversely, a secular politics of difference embraces complexity (in totality and exteriority) through historical reason and frequently manifests as participatory democracy. Whereas dogmatism's fate is tyranny, rationalism's destiny is democracy. The central thesis of *al-Maṣīr* is: "Ideas have wings. No one can prevent them from reaching people." While Ibn Rushd's fate was sealed by his exile and the burning of his books, his ideas were destined to remain relevant today because of the secular democratic function of poetic reason, which is inherently dialogical, for it is always a dance with the Other.

On the contrary, the dogmatist's false being is essentially monological. Historical reason, as the poetic path of desiring knowledge *qua* relative truth, is also the radical humanist engine of liberation praxis, which is a collective (i.e., democratic) process that inscribes equality "as a condition required for being able to think politics ... in the specific form of a particular case of dissensus" (Rancière, 2014, pp. 48–9). Transmodern liberation praxis is a pluriversal form of dissensus made possible through the dialogue between modernity and its alterity, which I have been articulating through my interpretations of the singularity of either Ibn Rushd or Chahine: the former's engagement with the Peripatetic school through Islamic philosophy and the latter's passion for (Euro-American) cinema through Arab poetics.

In sum, Chahine's transmodern cinema stretches modernity and humanism through a worlding of cinema that grounds modernity in Arab poetics and humanism in Islamic philosophy. Chahine accomplishes this cinematic worldliness with his aesthetics/poetics of liberation through a quantum leap from the singularity of his radical exteriority to the pluriversality of a secular democracy to come. In other words, Chahine's radical humanism, his dance with the Other, resignifies the Arab national project cinematically as an internationalist praxis of liberation, which delinks from all forms of oppression: capitalism, colonialism, imperialism, authoritarianism, fundamentalism, and so on.

Conclusion: The Future of Decolonial Film Theory

In a 1983 interview with Thierry Ardisson, Youssef Chahine, who was serving as a jury member, framed the Cannes Film Festival as a regional, as opposed to international, film festival because of its tokenistic inclusion of non-European films: "First of all, we are not interested in attending Cannes because we are not perceived as true partners; they do not care about our films, and they merely consider us as folklore." Chahine then expressed his disdain for the phrase "third world" when Ardisson was referring to the non-European world. Ardisson asked Chahine if there was a better phrase, and Chahine responded: "We are the Other; our existence is not less than their existence." Chahine added that dividing and ranking the world in terms of first, second, and third was absurd because while Euro-America may be leading technologically, it certainly is not a leader in terms of civilization.

I have been articulating this distinction throughout the book as the colonial difference between *the instrumental reason of oppressive modernization* and *the historical reason of liberatory modernity*. Technological modernization may be underdeveloped in the non-European world, but this does not deny the existence of an Other modernity with ancient roots, exemplified in the contributions of non-Europeans (e.g., Mesopotamians, Egyptians, Indians, Chinese) to human civilization. Suppose we follow both Chahine and Wahba that there is *one civilization with many cultures*. In that case, we must reject the designation "world cinema," particularly given the failure of the third world project.

Teshome Gabriel (1982) makes a compelling argument for the label "third cinema" as "a cinema of decolonization and for liberation" (p. 1). Inspired by Walter Benjamin's (1935) argument on the distinction between *the aestheticization of politics* under fascism and the antifascist *politicization of aesthetics*, Gabriel conceives third cinema as a praxis, or a material critique of ideology, "a confrontational cinema and an aesthetics of liberation" (p. 6). However, Gabriel does not cite Benjamin but refers to Frantz Fanon as "the inspirational guide for Third Cinema" (p. 7). Gabriel's argument is premised on the Fanonian axiom from *The Damned of the Earth*: "It is at the heart of *national consciousness* that *international consciousness* establishes itself and thrives" (Fanon, 1961/2004, p. 180, emphasis added).

If there is a universal, it is humanism; however, as a form of international consciousness, humanism will always manifest through the lens of culture as national consciousness. As such, we must speak of *radical humanisms* or the different revolutionary theories/practices of *secular criticism* from around the world that pertain to decolonial aesthetics, liberation ethics, and pluriversal politics (cf. Said, 1983). The error of liberal humanism is its assumption that Euro-Christian humanism is the only path to secularization, which speaks to the provincialism of its false universality.

Chahine's transmodern cinema embodies a radical vision of Arab modernity and Islamic humanism; his cinematic worldliness affirms the non-European Other in their exteriority. Chahine's dream of democratic secularization, which I have framed in terms of Arab internationalism, goes beyond the hegemony of both liberal humanism and conservative antihumanism. Liberal humanism's model of secularism is grounded in oppressive modernization, and conservative antihumanism's ideal (fundamentalism) is premised on sub-oppressive antimodernity.

Therefore, Chahine's radical humanism essentially prefigures transmodern worldhood by sublating the historical reason of the Other: national consciousness (liberatory modernity + historical reason) → international consciousness (world modernity + pluriversal politics). The trajectory of fascism, or authoritarianism more generally, is: ~~Other consciousness~~ → nationalist consciousness (modernization/colonization + instrumental reason). Other consciousness is barred as a function of the negation of the non-European Other (i.e., the Other of the Other).

Consequently, civilization or barbarism—even socialism or barbarism—may be reframed as *transmodernity or barbarism*. Barbarism is essentially a manifestation of instrumental reason, which employs unreason (cf. Wolin, 2004). It is no coincidence that the end of instrumental reason is a fascist politics of sameness; the means to this fascist politics range from colonialism to authoritarianism/fundamentalism. The external colonizer (oppressor) and the internal authoritarian/fundamentalist (sub-oppressor) share a tunnel vision commitment to dogmatism, wherein they believe they have exclusive access to the Absolute Truth, which justifies their authoritarian use of "reason" or unreason for the sake of domination. Instrumental reason is behind the genocidal logic employed by the Spanish Conquistadors, the Nazis, and contemporary terrorist groups like al-Qaeda and ISIL. This genocidal logic enacts a wish to exterminate difference (i.e., the Other of the Other).

Chahine's transmodern cinema rejects the genocidal logic of instrumental reason used by colonizers and authoritarians/fundamentalists; instead, Chahine presents his audience with a radical humanist vision expressed through decolonial aesthetics/poetics of liberation that are grounded in a secular democratic and pluriversal (read: antifascist) politics of difference. Furthermore, Chahine's celebration of human complexity is never at the expense of class struggle in society, which has been a central theme in his cinema since the 1950s. Echoing Fanon's argument, Khouri (2010) asserts that Chahine's personal/political cinema is not *only* about the unfinished Arab national project of liberation and self-determination but is also an aesthetic instantiation of this *nahḍa* project. As such, it is a revolutionary internationalist cinema, for it affirms the primacy of historical reason and the heterogeneity of Arab identity (cf. Khouri, 2010). Chahine's transmodern cinema eschews Euromodern colonialism, Islamic fundamentalism, and Arab fascism in one blow.

For Chahine, Arab national consciousness must be a *unity in diversity*—a unity based on a common language (Arabic) but comprised of diverse cultures and subjects. For him, the secular path toward radical humanism *qua* international consciousness is essentially socialist yet rooted in Islamic humanism and Arab modernity. If world cinema means an Other (or third) cinema that is considered less than Euro-American cinema, then *cinematic worldliness* signifies a counter-ideological internationalist cinema, which is genuinely committed to radical humanism and international (critical) consciousness. What is false consciousness but another name for dehumanization, which justifies the oppression and extermination of the non-European Other?

Some streaming service companies (e.g., Netflix) are doing a decent job of including films from around the world. For instance, Netflix added ten of Chahine's restored films to its platform. However, home video distribution companies (e.g., Criterion Collection) must better represent films from the African continent in general and the North African/West Asian region in particular. If our love, as cinephiles, is for enjoyable cinema and not ethnocentrism, then we must be dedicated to excellent films regardless of their country of origin. I feel passionate about African, Arab, and Egyptian cinemas specifically because I am an Egyptian subject committed to both pan-Africanism and pan-Arabism as liberation projects of unity in diversity. Still, my love for Egyptian cinema is not motivated solely by my Egyptianness, but more by the humanist values embodied in the decolonial aesthetics and transmodern poetics of radical Egyptian cinema.

The purpose of decolonial film theory is first to critique the coloniality of Euro-American cinema and film theory to shed light on the negated modernity of non-European cinema, which embodies an Other aesthetics/poetics that requires new forms of theorizing rooted in non-European histories and philosophies. The decolonial film theorist needs to think Otherwise about the aesthetics of liberation in decolonial cinema and ways of decolonizing Euro-American film theory, such as problematizing the "world cinema" label and demonstrating the erasure of non-European films in said theory; however, it is equally important not to equate modernity with modernization, or historical reason with instrumental reason, as I have argued throughout. Transmodernity is another term for *radical humanism as international (critical) consciousness*; to put it differently, the decolonial task entails accounting for the liberatory aesthetics and poetics of radical humanist cinema from around the world as pluriversal political embodiments of international critical consciousness.

I encourage non-European film theorists and filmmakers to continue resisting the cultural imperialism of Euro-American cinema and film theory through self-representation—this is the necessary work of delinking, border thinking, intercultural translation, and so on. The subaltern *can* speak in the language of cinema and they *can* make enjoyable films (i.e., masterpieces), which *can* raise our international critical consciousness through decolonial aesthetics and transmodern poetics of liberation. These liberatory aesthetics and poetics created in the exteriority of totality affirm the historical reason and radical humanism of non-European cinema, therefore its cinematic worldliness.

Following Wahba, if Ibn Rushd is a philosophical bridge over cultural difference, then Chahine is a cinematic bridge over colonial difference. Negating these bridges leads to perceiving difference as threatening, and without dialogue, we are only left with oppression and violence; Chahine's transmodern cinema affirms the importance of metaphorical bridges and celebrates the radical exteriority of the non-European Other. In the end, heretical ideas from totality's exteriority have wings, and no one—not even film theorists—can prevent them from reaching people. Therefore, the future of decolonial film theory is *transmodern cinema as the future*!

Further Reading on Youssef Chahine

Al-Aris, I. (2009). *Youssef Chahine: Nathrat al-tifl wa qabadat al-mutamarrid* [Youssef Chahine: The child's look and the rebel's fist]. Dar al-Shuruq.

Farid, S. (1997). *Adwa' 'ala sinimat Youssef Chahine* [Lights on Youssef Chahine's cinema]. Egyptian General Book Institute.

Fawal, I. (2001). *Youssef Chahine*. British Film Institute.

Gordon, J. (2002). *Revolutionary melodrama: Popular film and civic identity in Nasser's Egypt*. Middle East Documentation Center.

Gugler, J. (Ed.). (2011). *Film in the Middle East and North Africa: Creative dissidence*. University of Texas Press.

Khouri, M. (2010). *The Arab national project in Youssef Chahine's cinema*. American University in Cairo Press.

Massad, J. (1999). Art and politics in the cinema of Youssef Chahine. *Journal of Palestine Studies, 28*(2), 77–93.

Murphy, D., & Williams, P. (Eds.). (2007). *Postcolonial African cinema: Ten directors*. Manchester University Press.

Salama, M. (2018). *Islam and the culture of modern Egypt: From the monarchy to the Republic*. Cambridge University Press.

Shafik, V. (2007). *Arab cinema: History and cultural identity* (2nd ed.). American University in Cairo Press.

Shebl, M. (Director). (1995). *Hadoutet Chahine/Chahine's Story* (Docu-series, 12 episodes). Misr International Films.

Youssef Chahine's Filmography

1. 1950 بابا أمين *Papa Amin*
2. 1951 ابن النيل *Son of the Nile*
3. 1952 المهرج الكبير *The Great Clown*
4. 1952 سيدة القطار *Lady of the Train*
5. 1953 نساء بلا رجال *Women without Men*
6. 1954 صراع فى الوادي *Struggle in the Valley*
7. 1954 شيطان الصحراء *The Desert Devil*
8. 1956 صراع فى الميناء *Struggle in the Pier*
9. 1956 ودعت حبك *Farewell to Your Love*
10. 1957 إنت حبيبي *You're My Love*
11. 1958 باب الحديد *Cairo Station*
12. 1958 جميلة بوحريد *Jamila, the Algerian*
13. 1959 حب إلى الأبد *Eternal Love*
14. 1960 بين ايديك *In Your Hands*
15. 1960 نداء العشاق *A Lover's Call*
16. 1957 رجل في حياتي *A Man in My Life*
17. 1963 الناصر صلاح الدين *Saladin the Victorious*
18. 1965 فجر يوم جديد *Dawn of a New Day*
19. 1965 بياع الخواتم *The Ring Salesman*
20. 1967 عيد الميرون *The Feast of Mairun*
21. 1968 النيل الحياة *The Nile the Life*
22. 1970 الأرض *The Land*
23. 1971 الإختيار *The Choice*
24. 1971 رمال من ذهب *Golden Sands*
25. 1972 سلوى الفتاة الصغيرة التى تكلم الأبقار *Salwa the Little Girl Who Talks to Cows*
26. 1972 الناس والنيل *The People and the Nile*
27. 1972 العصفور *The Sparrow*
28. 1974 انطلاق *Forward We Go*
29. 1978 عودة الابن الضال *Return of the Prodigal Son*
30. 1979 إسكندرية... ليه؟ *Alexandria ... Why?*
31. 1982 حدوتة مصرية *An Egyptian Story*
32. 1985 وداعًا بونابرت *Adieu Bonaparte*

33.	1986	اليوم السادس *The Sixth Day*
34.	1989	إسكندرية كمان وكمان *Alexandria: Again and Forever*
35.	1991	القاهرة منورة بأهلها *Cairo as Told by Chahine*
36.	1994	المهاجر *The Emigrant*
37.	1997	المصير *The Destiny*
38.	1999	الأخر *The Other*
39.	2001	سكوت ح نصور *Silence, We're Rolling*
40.	2002	سبتمبر ١١ *September 11th*
41.	2004	إسكندرية-نيويورك *Alexandria-New York*
42.	2007	هي فوضى..؟ *Is This Chaos ...?*

References

Abdul-Jabbar, W. K. (2014). Towards a minor cinema: A Deleuzian reflection on Chahine's *Alexandria Why?* (1978). *Journal of North African Studies, 20*(2), 159–71. https://doi.org/10.1080/13629387.2014.917583.

Abu Zayd, N. H. (2004). *Rethinking the Qur'an: Towards a humanistic hermeneutics.* Humanistics University Press.

Adamson, P. (2016). *Philosophy in the Islamic world.* Oxford University Press.

Adonis. (1990). *An introduction to Arab poetics.* Saqi.

Adorno, T., Benjamin, W., Bloch, E., Brecht, B., & Lukács, G. (2010). *Aesthetics and politics.* Verso.

Ahmed, H. R. (2021). *The last Nahdawi: Taha Hussein and institution building in Egypt.* Stanford University Press.

Al-Azm, S. (2011). *Self-criticism after the defeat.* Saqi.

Al-Jabri, M. A. (1999). *Arab-Islamic philosophy.* University of Texas Press.

Al-Jabri, M. A. (2011). *The formation of Arab reason: Text, tradition and the construction of modernity in the Arab world.* Bloomsbury.

Al-Khalili, J. (2010). *The house of wisdom: How Arabic science saved ancient knowledge and gave us the renaissance.* Penguin.

Alcoff, L. M. (2020). Lugones's world-making. *Critical Philosophy of Race, 8*(1–2), 199–211. https://doi.org/10.5325/critphilrace.8.1-2.0199.

Alkassim, S., & Andary, N. (2018). *The cinema of Muhammad Malas: Visions of a Syrian auteur.* Springer.

Allen, T. W. (2012). *The invention of the white race. Volume 1: Racial oppression and social control.* Verso.

Amin, G. (2000). *Whatever happened to the Egyptians? Changes in Egyptian society from 1950 to the present.* American University in Cairo Press.

Amin, S. (1990). *Delinking: Towards a polycentric world.* Zed.

Andrew, J. D. (1976). *The major film theories: An introduction.* Oxford University Press.

Andrew, J. D. (1984). *Concepts in film theory.* Oxford University Press.

Ansary, T. (2009). *Destiny disrupted: A history of the world through Islamic eyes.* PublicAffairs.

Anzaldúa, G. (1987). *Borderlands: The new mestiza.* Aunt Lute.

Anzaldúa, G. (2015). *Light in the dark/Luz en Lo Oscuro: Rewriting identity, spirituality, reality*. Duke University Press.

Appiah, K. A. (2016, November 9). There is no such thing as Western civilisation. *The Guardian*. www.theguardian.com/world/2016/nov/09/western-civilisation-appiah-reith-lecture.

Aristotle. (1995). Poetics. In G. P. Goold (Ed.), *Loeb classical library 199* (S. Halliwell, Trans.) (pp. 1–141). Harvard University Press.

Arkoun, M. (2006). *Islam: To reform or to subvert?* Saqi.

Armes, R. (1981). Youssef Chahine and Egyptian cinema. *Framework, 14*(14), pp. 12–15.

Armes, R. (2015). *New voices in Arab cinema*. Indiana University Press.

Armes, R. (2018). *Roots of the new Arab film*. Indiana University Press.

Arnaldez, R. (2000). *Averroes: A rationalist in Islam*. Notre Dame Press.

Ballan, M. (2019). *The scribe of the Alhambra: Lisān al-Dīn Ibn al-Khatīb, sovereignty and history in Nasrid Granada* (Unpublished doctoral dissertation). University of Chicago.

Bauman, Z. (1989). *Modernity and the holocaust*. Polity Press.

Bedjaoui, A. (2020). *Cinema and the Algerian war of independence: Culture, politics, and society*. Springer.

Belkaïd, M. (2023). *From outlaw to rebel: Oppositional documentaries in contemporary Algeria*. Springer.

Benjamin, W. (1935/2006). The work of art in the age of its technological reproducibility. In *Walter Benjamin: Selected writings, 3: 1935–1938* (pp. 101–33). Belknap Press.

Berger, P. L. (1979). *The heretical imperative: Contemporary possibilities of religious affirmation*. Anchor Press/Doubleday.

Berman, M. (1988). *All that is solid melts into air: The experience of modernity*. Penguin.

Bernal, M. (1987). *Black Athena: The Afroasiatic roots of classical civilization. Volume I: The fabrication of Ancient Greece 1785–1985*. Rutgers University Press.

Beshara, R. K. (2019). *Decolonial psychoanalysis: Towards critical Islamophobia studies*. Routledge.

Beshara, R. K. (2021). *Freud and Said: Contrapuntal psychoanalysis as liberation praxis*. Palgrave Macmillan.

Bhabha, H. K. (1990). The third space. In J. Rutherford (Ed.), *Identity: Community, culture, difference* (pp. 207–21). Lawrence & Wishart.

Bhambra, G. K. (2014). Postcolonial and decolonial dialogues. *Postcolonial Studies*, *17*(2), 115–21. https://doi.org/10.1080/13688790.2014.966414.

Bloch, E. (2019). *Avicenna and the Aristotelian left*. Columbia University Press.

Borges, J. L. (1964). *Labyrinths: Selected stories & other writings*. New Directions.

Brody, R. (2020, August 21). What to stream: "Alexandria: Again and Forever," a masterpiece hiding on Netflix. *New Yorker*. www.newyorker.com/culture/the-front-row/what-to-stream-alexandria-again-and-forever-a-masterpiece-hiding-on-netflix.

Butler, J. (2016). *Frames of war: When is life grievable?* Verso.

Cazeaux, C. (Ed.). (2000). *The continental aesthetics reader*. Routledge.

Chambers, P. A. (2020). Epistemology and domination: Problems with the coloniality of knowledge thesis in Latin American decolonial theory. *Dados*, *63*(4). https://doi.org/10.1590/dados.2020.63.4.221.

Chaudhuri, S. (2022). *Crisis cinema in the Middle East: Creativity and constraint in Iran and the Arab World*. Bloomsbury.

Cousins, M. (2020). *The story of film*. Pavilion.

Critchley, S., & Webster, J. (2013). *The Hamlet doctrine*. Pantheon.

Curry, T. J. (2017). *The man-not: Race, class, genre, and the dilemmas of Black manhood*. Temple University Press.

Daifallah, Y. (2019). The politics of decolonial interpretation: Tradition and method in contemporary Arab thought. *American Political Science Review*, *113*(3), 810–23. https://doi.org/10.1017/s000305541900011x.

De Sousa Santos, B. (2014). *Epistemologies of the south: Justice against epistemicide*. Routledge.

Del Noce, A. (2014). *The crisis of modernity*. McGill-Queen's Press.

Deleuze, G. (1989). *Cinema 2: The time-image*. University of Minnesota Press.

Deleuze, G., & Guattari, F. (1986). *Kafka: Toward a minor literature*. University of Minnesota Press.

Dickinson, K. (2018). *Arab film and video manifestos: Forty-five years of the moving image amid revolution*. Springer.

Dickinson, K. (2019). *Arab cinema travels: Transnational Syria, Palestine, Dubai and beyond*. Bloomsbury.

Du Bois, W. E. (2007). *The souls of Black folk*. B. H. Edwards (Ed.). Oxford University Press.

Dussel, E. (1995). *The invention of the Americas: Eclipse of "the other" and the myth of modernity*. Continuum.

Dussel, E. (2009). A new age in the history of philosophy. *Philosophy & Social Criticism*, *35*(5), 499–516. https://doi.org/10.1177/0191453709103424.

Dussel, E. (2013). *Ethics of liberation: In the age of globalization and exclusion*. Duke University Press.

El-Ariss, T. (2013). *Trials of Arab modernity: Literary affects and the new political*. Fordham University Press.

Elsaket, I., Biltereyst, D., & Meers, P. (Eds.). (2023). *Cinema in the Arab world: New histories, new approaches*. Bloomsbury.

Ermarth, M. (1978). *Wilheim Dilthey: The critique of historical reason*. University of Chicago Press.

Escobar, A. (2007). Worlds and knowledges otherwise. *Cultural Studies*, *21*(2–3), 179–210. https://doi.org/10.1080/09502380601162506.

Escobar, A. (2020). *Pluriversal politics: The real and the possible*. Duke University Press.

Fakhry, M. (2001). *Averroes: His life, work and influence*. Oneworld.

Fakhry, M. (2004). *A history of Islamic philosophy*. Columbia University Press.

Fanon, F. (2004). *The wretched of the earth*. Grove/Atlantic.

Fanon, F. (2008). *Black skin, white masks*. Grove Press.

Fargeon, M. (1997, September). Interview: Youssef Chahine. *The UNESCO Courier*, 47–9.

Fawal, I. (2001). *Youssef Chahine*. British Film Institute.

Ferry, L. (2010). *A brief history of thought: A philosophical guide to living*. HarperCollins.

Finke, L. A., & Shichtman, M. B. (2015). Song, dance, and the politics of fanaticism: Youssef Chahine's destiny. *Screening the Past*, *41*. www.screeningthepast.com/issue-41-dossier/song-dance-and-the-politics-of-fanaticism-youssef-chahines-destiny.

Foucault, M. (1980). *Power/knowledge: Selected interviews and other writings, 1972–1977*. Vintage.

Freire, P. (1970). *Pedagogy of the oppressed*. Continuum.

Freud, S. (1939). *Moses and monotheism*. Hogarth Press.

Gabriel, T. H. (1982). *Third cinema in the third world: The aesthetics of liberation*. Umi Research Press.

Gaztambide, D. J. (2019). *A people's history of psychoanalysis: From Freud to liberation psychology*. Lexington.

References

Gaztambide-Fernández, R. (2014). Decolonial options and artistic/aestheSic entanglements: An interview with Walter Mignolo. *Decolonization: Indigeneity, Education & Society, 3*(1), 196–212.

Gibson, A. (2012). *Intermittency: The concept of historical reason in recent French philosophy.* Edinburgh University Press.

Giddens, A. (1990). *The consequences of modernity.* Polity.

Ginsberg, T. (2021). *Films of Arab Loutfi and Heiny Srour: Studies in Palestine solidarity cinema.* Springer.

Ginsberg, T., & Lippard, C. (Eds.). (2020). *Cinema of the Arab world: Contemporary directions in theory and practice.* Springer.

Goodman, L. E. (2003). *Islamic humanism.* Oxford University Press.

Grosfoguel, R. (2006). Preface. *Review (Fernand Braudel Center), 29*(2), 141–2.

Grosfoguel, R. (2011). Decolonizing post-colonial studies and paradigms of political-economy: Transmodernity, decolonial thinking, and global coloniality. *Transmodernity: Journal of Peripheral Cultural Production of the Luso-Hispanic World, 1*(1). https://doi.org/10.5070/t411000004.

Grosfoguel, R. (2013). The structure of knowledge in Westernised universities: Epistemic racism/sexism and the four genocides/epistemicides. *Human Architecture: Journal of the Sociology of Self-Knowledge, 1*(1), 73–90.

Gu, M. D. (2020). What is "decoloniality"? A postcolonial critique. *Postcolonial Studies, 23*(4), 596–600. https://doi.org/10.1080/13688790.2020.1751432.

Gugler, J. (Ed.). (2011). *Film in the Middle East and North Africa: Creative dissidence.* University of Texas Press.

Habti, D. (2011). Reason and revelation for an Averroist pursuit of Convivencia and intercultural dialogue. *Policy Futures in Education, 9*(1), 81–7. https://doi.org/10.2304/pfie.2011.9.1.81.

Hegel, G. W. (1975). *Lectures on the philosophy of world history.* Cambridge University Press.

Henry, P. (2000). *Caliban's reason: Introducing Afro-Caribbean philosophy.* Routledge.

Hoffman, D. (2007). Chahine's destiny: Prophetic nostalgia and the other middle ages. In L. T. Ramey & T. Pugh (Eds.), *Race, class, and gender in "medieval" cinema* (pp. 31–44). Palgrave Macmillan.

Hollis, J. (2009). *What matters most: Living a more considered life.* Gotham.

Horkheimer, M., & Adorno, T. W. (2002). *Dialectic of enlightenment.* Stanford University Press.

Horvath, R. J. (1972). A definition of colonialism. *Current Anthropology, 13*(1), 45–57. https://doi.org/10.1086/201248.

Hourani, A. (1991). *A history of the Arab peoples.* Belknap Press.

Hoyland, R. G. (2020). Were the Muslim Arab conquerors of the seventh-century Middle East colonialists? *Comparativ, 30*(3–4), 262–73.

Huntington, S. P. (1993). The clash of civilizations? *Foreign Affairs, 72*(3), 22. https://doi.org/10.2307/20045621.

Ibn Rushd. (2015). *On the harmony of religion and philosophy* (G. F. Hourani, Trans.). E. J. W. Gibb Memorial Trust.

Ismat, R. (2019). *Artists, writers and the Arab Spring.* Springer.

Jansen, J. C., & Osterhammel, J. (2017). *Decolonization: A short history.* Princeton University Press.

Josephson-Storm, J. A. (2017). *The myth of disenchantment: Magic, modernity, and the birth of the human sciences.* University of Chicago Press.

Kehr, D. (1996). The waters of Alexandria: The films of Youssef Chahine. *Film Comment, 32*(6), 23–7.

Kennedy, D. K. (2016). *Decolonization: A very short introduction.* Oxford University Press.

Khader, S. J. (2018). *Decolonizing universalism: A transnational feminist ethic.* Oxford University Press.

Khan, M. (1969). *An introduction to the Egyptian cinema.* Informatics.

Khatibi, A. (2019). *Plural Maghreb: Writings on postcolonialism.* Bloomsbury.

Khouri, M. (2010). *The Arab national project in Youssef Chahine's cinema.* American University in Cairo Press.

Kovel, J. (1970). *White racism: A psychohistory.* Pantheon.

Kracauer, S. (1997). *Theory of film: The redemption of physical reality.* Princeton University Press.

Lacoste, Y. (1984). *Ibn Khaldun: The birth of history and the past of the third world.* Verso.

Landau, J. M. (2016). *Studies in the Arab theater and cinema.* Routledge.

Lapsley, R., & Westlake, M. (1988). *Film theory: An introduction.* Manchester University Press.

Latour, B. (1993). *We have never been modern.* Harvard University Press.

Leaman, O. (1988). *Averroes and his philosophy.* Curzon.

Lekatsas, B. (2014). La pensée de midi: Mediterranean cosmopolitanism in the work of Camus, Cavafy, and Chahine. *Alif: Journal of Comparative Poetics, 34*, 125–50.

Limbrick, P. (2020). *Arab modernism as world cinema: The films of Moumen Smihi*. University of California Press.

Lugones, M. (2010). Toward a decolonial feminism. *Hypatia, 25*(4), 742–59. https://doi.org/10.1111/j.1527-2001.2010.01137.x.

Makdisi, U. (2023, January 3). Why Palestine is at the heart of what it means to be Arab. *Middle East Eye*. www.middleeasteye.net/opinion/palestine-heart-what-it-means-be-arab-why.

Maldonado-Torres, N. (2007). On the coloniality of being: Contributions to the development of a concept. *Cultural Studies, 21*(2–3), 240–70.

Maldonado-Torres, N. (2008). *Against war: Views from the underside of modernity*. Duke University Press.

Marcotte-Chenard, S. (2022). The critique of historical reason and the challenge of historicism. *Dialogue*, 1–22. https://doi.org/10.1017/s0012217322000233.

Marcuse, H. (1955). *Reason and revolution: Hegel and the rise of social theory* (2nd ed.). Routledge.

Massad, J. (1999). Art and politics in the cinema of Youssef Chahine. *Journal of Palestine Studies, 28*(2), 77–93. https://doi.org/10.2307/2537936.

Mast, G., Cohen, M., & Braudy, L. (Eds.). (1992). *Film theory and criticism: Introductory readings* (4th ed.). Oxford University Press.

Menocal, M. R. (2002). *The ornament of the world: How Muslims, Jews, and Christians created a culture of tolerance in medieval Spain*. Back Bay.

Mignolo, W. (2012). *Local histories/global designs: Coloniality, subaltern knowledges, and border thinking*. Princeton University Press.

Mignolo, W., & Vasquez, R. (2013). Decolonial aesthesis: Colonial wounds/decolonial healings. *Social Text*, n.p.

Mignolo, W. D. (2007). Delinking: The rhetoric of modernity, the logic of coloniality and the grammar of de-coloniality. *Cultural Studies, 21*(2–3), 449–514. https://doi.org/10.1080/09502380601162647.

Mignolo, W. D., & Tlostanova, M. V. (2006). Theorizing from the borders. *European Journal of Social Theory, 9*(2), 205–21. https://doi.org/10.1177/1368431006063333.

Mignolo, W. D., & Walsh, C. E. (2018). *On decoloniality: Concepts, analytics, praxis*. Duke University Press.

Miller, J. (2011). *Examined lives: From Socrates to Nietzsche*. Farrar, Straus and Giroux.

Murphy, D., & Williams, P. (2007). *Postcolonial African cinema: Ten directors*. Manchester University Press.

Nagib, L. (2006). Towards a positive definition of world cinema. In S. Dennison & S. H. Lim (Eds.), *Remapping world cinema: Identity, culture and politics in film* (pp. 30–7). Wallflower Press.

Najjar, F. M. (2004). Ibn Rushd (Averroes) and the Egyptian enlightenment movement. *British Journal of Middle Eastern Studies, 31*(2), 195–213. https://doi.org/10.1080/135301904042000268213.

Nkrumah, K. (1965). *Neo-colonialism: The last stage of imperialism*. International Publishers.

Ortega y Gasset, J. (1962). *History as a system: And other essays toward a philosophy of history*. W. W. Norton.

Ortega y Gasset, J. (1984). *Historical reason*. W. W. Norton.

Paquette, E. (2020). On Sylvia Wynter and feminist theory. *Philosophy Compass, 15*(12). https://doi.org/10.1111/phc3.12711.

Parker, J. (2020). Epistemology and decolonial politics. *Society and Space*. www.societyandspace.org/articles/epistemology-and-decolonial-politics.

Parvulescu, C. (2020). World cinema, VOD platforms and the Western demand. *Studies in World Cinema, 1*(1), 53–9. https://doi.org/10.1163/26659891-0000a001.

Ponzanesi, S., & Waller, M. (Eds.). (2012). *Postcolonial cinema studies*. Routledge.

Prashad, V. (2007). *The darker nations: A people's history of the third world*. New Press.

Puerta Vílchez, J. M. (2017). *Aesthetics in Arabic thought: From pre-Islamic Arabia through Al-Andalus*. Brill.

Quijano, A. (1989). Paradoxes of modernity in Latin America. *International Journal of Politics, Culture and Society, 3*(2), 147–77. https://doi.org/10.1007/bf01387928.

Quijano, A. (1993). Modernity, identity, and utopia in Latin America. *boundary 2, 20*(3), 140. https://doi.org/10.2307/303346.

Quijano, A. (2000). Coloniality of power and eurocentrism in Latin America. *International Sociology, 15*(2), 215–32. https://doi.org/10.1177/0268580900015002005.

Quijano, A. (2007). Coloniality and modernity/rationality. *Cultural Studies, 21*(2–3), 168–78. https://doi.org/10.1080/09502380601164353.

Rakha, Y. (2020). *Barra and Zaman: Reading Egyptian modernity in Shadi Abdel Salam's The Mummy*. Springer.

Ramos, J. G. (2018). *Sensing decolonial aesthetics in Latin American arts*. University Press of Florida.

Rancière, J. (2004). *The politics of aesthetics*. Bloomsbury.

Rancière, J. (2014). *Dissensus: On politics and aesthetics*. Bloomsbury.

Rojas-Sotelo, M. (2014). Decolonizing aesthetics. In M. Kelly (Ed.), *Encyclopedia of aesthetics* (2nd ed., pp. 300–4). Oxford University Press.

Russell, B. (1945). *History of Western philosophy*. Simon & Schuster.

Said, E. W. (1978). *Orientalism*. Penguin.

Said, E. W. (1983). *The world, the text, and the critic*. Harvard University Press.

Said, E. W. (1993). *Culture and imperialism*. Vintage.

Said, E. W. (1994). *Representations of the intellectual*. Vintage.

Said, E. W. (2001, October 4). The clash of ignorance. *The Nation*. www.thenation.com/article/archive/clash-ignorance.

Said, E. W. (2003). *Freud and the non-European*. Verso.

Said, E. W. (2004). *Humanism and democratic criticism*. Columbia University Press.

Salama, M. (2018). *Islam and the culture of modern Egypt: From the monarchy to the republic*. Cambridge University Press.

Shabout, N. M. (2007). *Modern Arab art: Formation of Arab aesthetics*. University Press of Florida.

Shafik (2021, May 14). *Definition of decolonising cinema with Viola Shafik, filmmaker and scholar*. YouTube. www.youtube.com/watch?v=c0nhyyrBe3E.

Shafik, V. (1998/2017). *Arab cinema: History and cultural identity* (2nd ed.). American University in Cairo Press.

Shafik, V. (2007). *Popular Egyptian cinema: Gender, class, and nation*. American University in Cairo Press.

Shafik, V. (2015). Youssef Chahine: Devouring mimicries or juggling with self and other (Egypt). In J. Gugler (Ed.), *Ten Arab filmmakers: Political dissent and social critique* (pp. 99–120). Indiana University Press.

Shaheen, J. G. (2001). *Reel bad Arabs: How Hollywood vilifies a people*. Olive Branch Press.

Sheehi, S. (2004). *Foundations of modern Arab identity*. University Press of Florida.

Shepard, T. (2015). *Voices of decolonization: A brief history with documents*. St. Martin's.

Shohat, E., & Stam, R. (2014). *Unthinking Eurocentrism: Multiculturalism and the media*. Routledge.

Solomon, R. C., & Higgins, K. M. (1996). *A short history of philosophy*. Oxford University Press.

Stam, R. (2000). *Film theory: An introduction*. Blackwell.

Stam, R. (2023). *Indigeneity and the decolonizing gaze: Transnational imaginaries, media aesthetics, and social thought*. Bloomsbury.

Stromback, D. (2019). Is there a post-Marxist criticism to the decolonial critique? *Journal of Decolonising Disciplines, 1*(2), 121–42. https://doi.org/10.35293/jdd.v1i2.24.

Táíwò, O. (2022). *Against decolonisation: Taking African agency seriously.* Hurst.

Tamamy, S. M. (2014). *Averroes, Kant and the origins of the enlightenment: Reason and revelation in Arab thought.* Bloomsbury.

Taylor, R. (2009). Ibn Rushd/Averroes and "Islamic" rationalism. *Medieval Encounters, 15*(2–4), 225–35. https://doi.org/10.1163/157006709x458837.

Thakur, G. B. (2015). *Postcolonial theory and avatar.* Bloomsbury.

Thiong'o, N. W. (1986). *Decolonising the mind: The politics of language in African literature.* East African Educational Publishers.

Tibi, B. (2012). Islamic humanism vs. Islamism: Cross-civilizational bridging. *Soundings: An Interdisciplinary Journal, 95*(3), 230–54. https://doi.org/10.5325/soundings.95.3.0230.

Touraine, A. (1995). *Critique of modernity.* Wiley-Blackwell.

Trouillot, M. R. (1995). *Silencing the past: Power and the production of history.* Beacon Press.

Tuck, E., & Yang, K. W. (2012). Decolonization is not a metaphor. *Decolonization: Indigeneity, Education & Society, 1*(1), 1–40.

Urvoy, D. (1991). *Ibn Rushd (Averroes).* Routledge.

Vallega, A. A. (2014a). *Latin American philosophy from identity to radical exteriority.* Indiana University Press.

Vallega, A. A. (2014b). Exordio/Exordium: For an aesthetics of liberation out of Latin American experience. *Symposium, 18*(1), 125–40. https://doi.org/10.5840/sympos ium20141817.

Vázquez, R. (2020). *Vistas of modernity: Decolonial aesthesis and the end of the contemporary.* Mondriaan Fund.

Vergès, F. (2021). *A decolonial feminism.* Pluto Press.

Von Kügelgen, A. (1996). A call for rationalism: "Arab Averroists" in the twentieth century. *Alif: Journal of Comparative Poetics, 16*, 97–132. https://doi.org/10.2307/521832.

Wagner, M. S. (2022, November 25). The "Arab awakening": A popular but dubious myth. *New Lines Magazine.* https://newlinesmag.com/essays/nahda-arab-awaken ing-a-popular-but-dubious-myth.

Wahba, M. (1980). The paradox of Averroes. *Archiv für Rechts- und Sozialphilosophie, 66*(2), 257–60. www.jstor.org/stable/23679473.

Wahba, M. (2006). Averroes as a bridge. *Think*, *4*(12), 13–16. https://doi.org/10.1017/s1477175600001652.

Wahba, M. (2022). *Fundamentalism and secularization* (R. K. Beshara, Trans.). Bloomsbury.

Wahba, M., & Abousenna, M. (Eds.). (2010). *Averroes and the enlightenment*. Prometheus.

Weaver-Hightower, R., & Hulme, P. (Eds.). (2014). *Postcolonial film: History, empire, resistance*. Routledge.

Williams, P. (2014). Al Masir/destiny (Youssef Chahine, 1997): "a luta continua." In L. Bisschoff & D. Murphy (Eds.), *Africa's lost classics: New histories of African cinema*. Legenda.

Wolin, R. (2004). *The seduction of unreason: The intellectual romance with fascism from Nietzsche to postmodernism*. Princeton University Press.

Wynter, S. (2003). Unsettling the coloniality of being/power/truth/freedom: Towards the human, after man, its overrepresentation—An argument. *CR: The New Centennial Review*, *3*(3), 257–337. https://doi.org/10.1353/ncr.2004.0015.

Žižek, S. (2000). De capo senza fine. In J. Butler, E. Laclau, & S. Žižek (Eds.), *Contingency, hegemony, universality: Contemporary dialogues on the left*. Verso.

Index

Adonis 4, 63, 68–9, 78, 163
Africa 2, 4, 11, 18–19, 21, 32, 34, 46, 66, 70, 74, 99, 103–4, 108–9, 119, 123
African cinema 99, 103–4, 107–9, 115
aísthēsis 62, 64–6, 85, 92–3
Amin, Samir 15, 45, 47
anachronic temporality 63, 68–9, 71, 78, 90, 119, 141, 148
al-Andalus 5, 22, 34, 37, 42, 56, 60, 66, 69, 70, 79, 87, 113, 133, 139, 147
anticolonial 21, 46, 100, 104, 107, 118, 120, 138, 146
Anzaldúa, Gloria 12, 45, 47, 69–70
Arab cinema 4, 6–7, 70, 99, 115–19, 123
Arab modernity 63, 68, 71–2, 87, 90, 138, 142, 146–7, 154, 156
Arabs 7, 22, 37, 69–71, 78, 80, 86, 103, 117, 119, 128, 140
Aristotle 62, 79, 81–2, 87, 89–95, 97, 149
authoritarian(ism) 5, 21–3, 27, 46, 50, 55, 71, 84, 118, 120, 126, 133, 135–6, 141, 145, 147–8, 151–2, 154–5

biography 17, 51, 87, 91, 99, 101, 107, 113–14, 117–19, 125–6, 128, 131, 141, 149
Bloch, Ernst 63, 91
border thinking 3–4, 11–2, 23, 35, 44–8, 51, 58, 60, 66, 69–71, 80–2, 85–7, 91–2, 94, 96–7, 102, 109–10, 113, 129, 138–9, 146, 157
borderland spatiality 69, 71, 139

capitalism 4, 6, 10, 14, 16, 18, 28, 30, 33, 35–8, 40, 43–4, 47, 57, 59, 61, 71–3, 79, 92, 99–100, 112, 118, 126, 128, 131, 138, 141, 145, 147, 152
Chahine, Youssef 1–8, 17, 21–4, 27, 44, 46, 48–51, 55–6, 61, 63–4, 66, 72–4, 82, 86–7, 91–2, 96, 99–103, 105–15, 117–29, 131, 133, 135–7, 139–42, 144, 146–57

cinematic worldliness 8–9, 55, 72, 103, 109, 115, 125, 129, 146–7, 152, 154, 156–7
civilization 2, 7–8, 31–2, 34–5, 37, 39, 44, 49–50, 57, 60–1, 66–7, 73–4, 80, 83, 85–6, 92, 100, 112, 137, 139, 143, 148, 153, 155
class 4, 33, 35–6, 38, 67, 72–3, 95, 99–100, 112, 115, 118, 131, 145, 155
colonial difference 2–3, 16, 37, 44, 48, 61, 73, 143, 153, 157
colonialism 3, 9–13, 18, 20, 33, 36–8, 41, 47, 57, 59, 70–1, 73–4, 99, 107, 118, 120, 141, 152, 155
coloniality 2–3, 5, 10, 12–16, 20, 29, 31, 33, 35–40, 42–7, 49, 52, 67, 73–4, 90, 103, 111, 140, 143, 145, 148, 156
colonization 2, 14–15, 23, 28, 31, 33, 40–1, 43–4, 83, 107, 138, 140, 147–8, 154
Córdoba 56, 79, 87, 89, 131, 134–5, 139
cosmopolitan(ism) 3, 5, 44, 51, 57, 66, 80, 82, 85, 92, 96, 103, 125, 129, 168

decolonial film theory 1, 3, 11–12, 22–4, 66, 72–4, 102, 137–8, 143, 146, 156–7
decoloniality 3, 9, 11, 13, 18–20, 24, 42, 46, 51, 55, 61, 68–70, 72, 145–7
decolonization 2, 6, 9–11, 17–21, 46, 61, 71, 74, 115, 126, 154
Deleuze, Gilles 100–3, 109
delinking 9, 12, 15, 23, 45–7, 65, 87, 96, 102–3, 111, 117, 126, 138, 145–6, 152, 157
democracy 7, 22, 49–50, 55–6, 59, 79, 96, 100, 103, 112–13, 115, 136, 148, 151–2, 154–5
Descartes, René 20, 41, 44, 57, 66, 84–5, 94
destiny 1, 53, 97, 111, 129, 150–1
dialectic 1–2, 5, 12, 17, 19, 22, 27, 30–4, 49, 52, 54, 67–8, 81, 92, 95–6, 112, 125, 128, 131

Index

dialogue 2, 11, 16, 28, 50, 60–1, 69, 73, 82, 86, 96, 103, 111, 125, 141, 151, 157

discourse 2, 8–9, 14, 31, 36, 44, 52, 60, 72, 83, 89, 95, 97, 118, 137, 149

Dussel, Enrique 4, 9–11, 13, 19, 30–4, 41–2, 46, 49–50, 52, 67, 86

Egyptian cinema 1, 3, 6, 8, 64, 99, 103, 115–16, 120–4, 126, 140, 156

Eurocentrism 5, 10, 12, 14–15, 31–2, 34–5, 39–41, 67, 73, 111, 137, 144, 148

Euromodern(ity) 2, 4–5, 17, 30, 32, 34, 38, 40–1, 44, 46, 48–9, 55–6, 66–9, 73, 82, 90, 102, 138, 146, 155

exteriority 1–5, 8–9, 12, 19–20, 22–4, 31–4, 44, 46, 48–9, 60–1, 64–6, 68–9, 71–3, 82, 87, 102, 109, 111, 114, 125, 129, 137–9, 143–4, 146–47, 151–2, 154, 157

Fakhry, Majid 78, 80–2, 84–5, 87, 89–90, 149–51

Fanon, Frantz 10–12, 20, 36, 43–4, 66, 107, 154–5, 166

Fawal, Ibrahim 1, 4, 119, 122, 125–9

fundamentalism 5, 22–3, 27–8, 70–1, 78–9, 81, 84, 92, 96, 110, 112, 116, 118, 120, 126, 128, 131–6, 139, 141–2, 145, 147–8, 150–2, 155

Global South 4–6, 10–11, 32–3, 46–8, 55, 57, 60, 72, 74, 99–100, 123, 144

Hegel, G. W. F. 52–3, 96, 100, 145

hegemony 3, 7, 34, 41–2, 45, 51, 58, 66, 72, 74, 81, 84, 94, 103, 120, 154

historical reason 4–5, 14–5, 21, 28, 31, 34, 42, 46, 49, 51–55, 57, 61, 66, 69, 73, 83, 85, 92, 96–7, 111–13, 129, 136, 138, 140–1, 143, 146–7, 150–1, 153–7

humanism 15, 22–3, 29, 54–5, 61, 71, 74, 78, 81, 83–6, 89, 91–3, 95–6, 102, 111–13, 125–6, 129, 135, 139, 141, 146, 148, 152, 154–7

Ibn Rushd 23–4, 40–1, 44, 55, 57, 60–1, 69, 73–4, 77–97, 111, 113, 131, 133–7, 142, 146, 149–51, 157

ideology 3–4, 7, 9, 12–4, 17–21, 29, 33–4, 36, 38, 48, 60, 66–7, 69, 73, 78, 81, 83, 86, 92, 100, 104, 107–8, 112, 116–17, 127–8, 137, 142, 145, 147, 154, 156

Indigenous 2–3, 18, 23, 33, 37–9, 42, 56, 59, 74

instrumental reason 14–5, 22, 31, 35, 42, 49, 52, 66, 73, 79, 112, 136, 143, 153, 155–6

(inter)nationalism 4, 22, 28, 55–6, 61, 70–1, 83, 100, 116–18, 120, 122, 127, 133, 139, 148, 152, 154–6

intercultural translation 2, 58–61, 80, 82, 86, 103, 138, 141, 146, 157

Islam 22, 34, 40, 69–70, 81–3, 86, 92, 96, 110, 119, 150

Islamic philosophy 77, 79, 81, 86, 90, 92, 96, 152

Khouri, Malek 1, 4, 139–42, 155

Latin America 2, 4, 9–10, 13–14, 19–20, 32, 52, 67, 165

liberation ethics 1, 4, 12, 50, 87, 113, 141, 154

Maldonado-Torres, Nelson 12–3, 43–4

al-Maṣīr 1, 3–5, 7–8, 22–4, 27, 34, 56, 61, 64, 72–3, 75–152

minor cinema 99–101

modern/colonial 4–5, 13, 16, 35, 45, 55–6, 65, 137, 143

modernity 4–5, 10, 12–6, 19, 21, 23, 27–37, 40, 42–6, 49–52, 54, 58, 60, 62–4, 68, 71–3, 78, 83–4, 87, 90, 111–12, 116, 138–43, 145–8, 151–4, 156

modernization 14–15, 21–2, 27, 29–31, 33, 35, 42, 52, 57, 66–8, 78, 84, 100, 112, 140, 147–8, 153–4, 156

al-nahḍa 68, 82–3, 150, 155

Nasser, Gamal Abdel 22, 100, 110, 119–20, 122, 125, 127

negation 1–4, 7, 9, 23, 31–3, 40–1, 44, 48–9, 55, 66, 72, 82, 85, 100, 124, 129, 138, 142–3, 150–1, 155–7 oppression 23, 27, 30–5, 43, 46, 50–1, 55, 57, 61, 67, 73, 84, 87, 100, 107, 112–13, 124, 126, 128, 140, 145–8, 152–7

Orientalism 32, 34, 39, 48, 71, 74, 90, 92, 109–11, 116–17, 123, 137–40

Other 1, 3–4, 11, 23, 30–2, 34, 49–52, 61, 71–2, 82, 92, 96, 111–14, 129, 142, 144, 151–5

particularity 6, 8, 19–20, 53, 92

pluriversality 1, 4–5, 8, 19, 23, 41, 45–7, 50–1, 54–6, 65–6, 71, 83, 85, 87, 94, 96, 102–3, 109, 112–13, 116, 125, 129, 139, 142, 146–8, 150–52, 154–6

poetics 63–5, 68, 70–1, 78, 83, 87, 92–3, 131–52, 155–7

poiēsis 62, 64, 82, 85, 93, 127

politics of difference 2, 71, 103, 113–15, 151, 155

postcoloniality 3, 9–12, 18–20, 46–7, 100, 103–4, 107–8, 116–18, 120, 127–8, 145

postmodernity 19, 28, 31, 37, 49, 52, 128

praxis 2–3, 9, 12, 17, 19, 27, 44, 49–51, 61, 70, 87, 102, 126, 138, 141–2, 151–2, 154

Quijano, Aníbal 4, 9–11, 13–15, 20, 28, 30–1, 35–6, 38–40, 42, 45, 51–3, 67–8

racism 2, 6, 13, 16, 29, 34, 38, 42–3, 47, 56, 67, 77, 85

Rancière, Jacques 52, 62–5, 151

representation 6–7. 12. 17, 41, 48, 55, 62, 93, 108–9, 116, 129, 137–9, 141, 144, 146, 149, 157

revolution 19, 50, 53, 63, 100–1, 110, 113, 117, 120, 126–8, 145, 154–5

Said, Edward 2, 8–12, 20, 34, 36, 38, 41, 46–8, 54, 85, 91–2, 108–9, 111–12, 115, 125–6, 138–40, 154

secular 5, 8, 22, 27–30, 40, 54, 70–1, 81–6, 91–2, 94, 96, 102, 110–12, 120, 131–2, 135–6, 142, 147–8, 151–2, 154–5

Shafik, Viola 4, 74, 112, 116–24

singularity 8, 51, 55, 62, 66, 71, 92, 99, 102, 109, 115–16, 125–6, 129, 151–2

socialism 22, 47, 100, 117, 120, 126–7, 155–6

spatiality 66, 69–71, 73, 139

subjectivity 2, 16, 28, 33–4, 40–1, 44, 49, 51, 54–5, 58, 63, 70, 78, 83–5, 102, 125, 129, 140, 147

temporality 39–40, 62–3, 66–9, 71, 73, 78, 90, 94, 96, 119, 141, 148

third-world 6, 46–7, 51, 99–102, 108, 144–7, 153

totality 1–3, 5, 8–9, 12, 19, 22, 31–2, 49, 61, 64, 72–3, 82, 87, 102, 111, 129, 144, 147, 151, 157

transmodern cinema 1, 8–9, 12, 24, 44, 46, 50, 55, 73–4, 86, 100–1, 103, 114, 124, 126, 129, 135, 145–8, 152, 154, 157

transmodernity 12, 15, 23, 27, 31–4, 41, 49–50, 52, 60, 72, 103, 116, 143, 147, 155–6

unconscious 14, 32, 37, 40, 44, 48, 66, 71–2, 86, 125, 141, 145, 147

universality 6, 8–9, 11, 16–17, 19–20, 45–6, 53, 55, 59, 65, 74, 84–5, 91–5, 147, 150, 154

Vallega, Alejandro 4, 65, 67–8, 71, 140

violence 4, 17, 27, 30, 35, 43, 51, 55, 61, 67, 73, 133, 137, 140–2, 145–6, 157

Wahba, Mourad 61, 66, 84, 86, 90, 92, 96, 112, 128, 135, 149–50, 153, 157

west(ern) 5, 13–5, 17, 21, 38–40, 45, 58–9, 61, 65, 67, 69–72, 74, 77, 81, 83, 85, 86, 92, 104, 107–10, 112, 119, 122–4, 139–40, 144, 156

world cinema 5–7, 55, 73–4, 99–101, 116, 145–7, 153, 156

Milton Keynes UK
Ingram Content Group UK Ltd.
UKHW051305170724
7UKWH00005B/11